WORLD BEAT

A LISTENER'S GUIDE
TO CONTEMPORARY
WORLD MUSIC ON CD

PETER SPENCER

A CAPPELLA BOOKS

Library of Congress Cataloging-in-Publication Data

Spencer, Peter, 1951–
    World beat : a listener's guide to contemporary world music
    on CD / Peter Spencer.
            p.   cm.
    Includes bibliographical references.
    ISBN 1-55652-140-5 : $12.95
    1. Popular music—Compact disc catalogs. I. Title.

    ML156.4.P6S7   1992
    016.78163'0266—dc20   91-45607
                                                          CIP
                                                          MN

Published in 1992 by
a cappella books, incorporated
5 4 3 2 1

Printed in the United States of America

Editorial offices:
PO Box 380
Pennington, NJ 08534

Business/sales offices:
814 N. Franklin St.
Chicago, IL 60610

Cover design by Christine Ronan

To
Leyla Özbekhan Spencer

Sister, let me tell you
About a vision that I saw.
—Bob Dylan, from *Precious Angel*

Contents

Acknowledgments VII

Introduction 1

1 Southern Africa 7

2 Western Africa 21

3 Northern and Eastern Africa 39

4 Eastern Europe 49

5 Western Europe 65

6 The Caribbean Islands 81

7 North America 105

8 South America 125

9 India and Australasia 133

Afterword 143

Appendix A: Mail-Order Addresses 145

Appendix B: Retail Record Stores 151

Bibliography 159

Acknowledgments

I SHOULD BEGIN BY thanking Tim Quinn and Kris Jesson, whose willingness to let me write about this music in the pages of the Trenton *Times* started the whole process and whose understanding and friendship have kept me alive over the last few years. Another must-name is Richard Carlin, the most sympathetic and understanding of editors. I doubt if I could have produced this volume for anybody else.

There were many people whose opinions and expertise informed the project as I went along. My thanks go to Hayes Ferguson, Cajun-in-residence at the *Times;* Dave Van Ronk, a great teacher and intellect; John Leonard, who showed me just how high the stakes are; and Daisann McLane, the first person I knew who listened to and wrote about world music and somebody whom I remain pathetically eager to impress. Randy Alexander, at the *Times'* pop-music desk, generously provided me with contacts and releases.

Special thanks go to my lovely sister-in-law Ayshe Özbekhan for lending me so many of her favorite albums, or simply reading their catalogue numbers to me over the telephone late at night. And my patient father-in-law Hassan Özbekhan has been an ongoing reference to Turkish culture for many years.

Although there are plenty of reference books listed in the bibliography, I feel the need to acknowledge one source in particular. It may only be a fifty-page pamphlet, but I probably used the listener's guide to the National Public Radio program "Afro-pop Worldwide" as much as any other single work. This valuable booklet is available by mail, free with SASE, from World Music Productions, 131 Park Place, Brooklyn, New York 11217.

Certainly the most materially helpful people throughout the whole process were those record company executives who believed in the project and were willing to help. I found again and again that the companies that offered the most enthusiasm and assistance always seemed to be the ones with the best music and the most thorough knowledge of it. I am especially grateful for the advice, friendship, and support of Carrie Ann Svingen at Rykodisc, Andrew Seidenfeld at Shanachie, Ellen Battle at Mango, Chris Strachwitz at Arhoolie, Mike Fleischer at Flying Fish, and Glenn Dicker at Rounder.

Finally, it needs to be said that my wife was a rock throughout. She made so many material, editorial, and moral contributions that they cannot be adequately detailed. Her favorite phrase—it became almost a mantra—was, "You'll finish this book if it's the last thing I do!"

God bless you all.

Introduction

PAUL SIMON MAY BE the best-known pop musician currently finding inspiration in the music of other countries, but the list of American and British artists who use world music to bring new freshness to their work is getting longer all the time. Peter Gabriel's commitment to the form includes the formation of a record company, RealWorld, with one of the most diversified catalogues in the business. David Byrne, both by himself and with his group, Talking Heads, has become a walking desk-reference of African and South American styles. Poi Dog Pondering and 3 Mustaphas 3 are two of a new generation of bands for whom world music has become second nature.

And in the same way that pop fans in the sixties went looking for the early blues records that had nourished favorite groups like Cream and the Rolling Stones, so today's discerning listeners are searching out and discovering the incredible variety of indigenous musics from around the world, led by those American and British artists at the cutting edge of this trend.

Record companies, especially independent, progressive labels like Rounder, Shanachie, and Rykodisc, are finding that world music albums are becoming their most popular releases. The radio stations serviced by these companies are finding that more and more listeners want to hear the music of Africa, India, South America, Eastern Europe, the Arab world, Asia, and Australia. They respond with more shows dedicated to world music, including at least one nationally syndicated program, "Afro-pop Worldwide," hosted by the Senegalese DJ Georges Collinet.

Most major cities now have at least one top-flight nightclub booking world-music bands seven nights a week, and groups from the thriving European world-pop scene are finding that they can book long tours across the United States and play to large, enthusiastic audiences. As if to symbolize this unprecedented acceptance, the South African group Ladysmith Black Mambazo appears regularly on television's "Sesame Street."

So let's say you are a *discerning* fan of popular music. You enjoy music that makes you dance and think at the same time or, saving that, music that at least goes out of its way to keep you from feeling like a laboratory rat. But as time goes by you find less and less popular music that you want to listen to. The "experimental" types begin to sound studied, major figures are repeating themselves, the rock bands get stupider every year, and soul music is gone, replaced either by slick, insincere balladeers or by rap, which seems to be mostly bragging about rape.

So you decide you'll just stick with your old favorites: maybe Dylan or Jackson Browne, Elvis Costello or Talking Heads, Led Zeppelin or Jimi Hendrix, John Coltrane or Bobby Short or Otis Redding. But you always hated the people who just listened to one thing their whole lives and, besides, music serves different purposes for you these days. Instead of sitting in your room alone, howling at the moon with Neil Young, you prefer having friends come over to your house for dinner or drinks or just to spend time. Nowadays the music you play needs to be sophisticated but not obtrusive, easy to take but not at all bland, unfamiliar without being patronizing.

World music gives the American listener a sense of freedom from the constraints of standardized Anglo-American pop, without the arid, over-intellectual pomposity of much "progressive" music. World music is both entertaining and different. It takes the listener to a place where the world's various cultures meet happily and in the spirit of festival. It is a force for understanding and goodwill in an increasingly dark world.

That sounds good, but the world is a big place, and the search for new music from other countries can be daunting. There are so many releases, so many regional styles to choose from, and nobody can be expected to listen to everything. That is where this book comes in. As one can tell by its heft, this is not an encyclopaedia. Nor is it an ethnomusicological treatise or a work of music history. I have no particular interest in laying claim to the title The Guy Who Knows Everything. This book is designed with the first-time buyer in mind, someone who wants to get into world music but would like to know where to start, who is not absolutely made of money, and would like to be sure that each CD they are buying is something that will bear repeated listening.

There will be few bad reviews in this volume. My feeling has always been that the best way to treat indifferent music is to ignore it. It always goes away eventually. Besides, more readers will be interested in which world-music CDs are worth buying than in which ones are not. Of course, the fact remains that there will be some forms or regional styles that I enjoy less than others. Feel free to try and spot any lapses of enthusiasm and, if you find one, you have my permission to buy me dinner and laugh at me while I eat your food.

The text will divide the world into nine not always distinct or even logically defensible regions—Southern Africa, Western Africa, Northern and Eastern Africa, Eastern Europe, Western Europe, the Caribbean Islands, North America,

South America, and India and Australasia—with a chapter devoted to each. Chapters will survey CDs released in the United States, using the *Schwann* catalogue as the final authority on whether something is or is not in print. For those of you who are not familiar with it, the *Schwann* catalogue is the leading record-industry publication listing in-print LPs, CDs, and cassettes. It is generally recognized as an authoritative source for the industry. We will survey both the indigenous or "folk" music of these regions and the popular music that is in its essence a regionalized reworking of Anglo-American pop—or an Anglo-Americanized reworking of regional pop. Each chapter ends with a complete list of the CDs discussed in it, with highly recommended items highlighted to guide the beginning listener.

Naturally, some "judgment calls" will have to be made. For example, the musics of India and Brazil have both been mined fairly extensively by American jazz musicians. Basically, anything that sounds too familiar will be left out. The various jazz fusions have many chroniclers more adept than I. For much the same reason, the North American and European sections will not deal with rock and roll, not because it isn't a vernacular music (it obviously is) and not because it does not connect with its listeners on a "tribal" level (it obviously does, at least much of the time), but because its wide acceptance has made what was once a format-busting fusion of styles into the most rigid format yet. And the ripple effect of rock's extraordinary popularity affects the vernacular musics out of which it arose—blues, country, gospel, and jazz, among others—placing them, too, outside the bounds of this survey. There are still some vernacular musics left in North America (most of them tied to non-English-speaking regional cultures), and we will look at them even if they have been touched by establishment forms—as in the case of Louisiana's Cajun music and *zydeco*.

What these judgment calls boil down to is not really a "definition" of what is or is not an indigenous form. It is more of a gut feeling on the part of the listener. To elaborate: When

Muddy Waters' "Louisiana Blues" first came out early in 1951, the rhythm and blues charts were completely dominated by slick ballads and sophisticated, jazzy "jump" blues. And people in Hell, the saying goes, want ice water. The Mississippi style of Waters and others struck a deep chord in urban blacks who had left the South in recent years—it was the rough and unpolished sound of home. It made a statement to them about who they were, where they had come from, and what their relationship really was with the media establishment. It was music that had not been imposed on them, but had arisen out of their own community in a way that left most of the pop music of the day sounding limp and meaningless.

Of course, it's a safe bet that the music of Jali Musa Jawara did not arise from any community within the range of this book's distribution. But the bond that a vernacular music has with its particular subculture is something that can be felt even by those outside of the subculture—witness the worldwide reverence given to Muddy Waters. And for the American listener who defines his or her taste by its unorthodoxy, discovering music that expresses that distance—be it Beausoleil, the Sabri Brothers, or the Boyoyo Boys—is one of the moments that makes life real. This book intends to facilitate that process.

For most of this century, the United States has broadcast its collective musical genius around the world. At first we got dim, then increasingly strong echoes back from Europe; but now a giant wave is building, as the musicians of the entire world begin to show us what they've added to that genius. The music of the next century is on its way to us now. Good hunting!

Ladysmith Black Mambazo. *Courtesy Shanachie Records*

1

〰〰〰〰〰〰〰〰〰〰〰

SOUTHERN
AFRICA

FOR MOST AMERICAN LISTENERS, "world music" *begins* in
Southern Africa. Many got their first inkling that American
pop was being given a new twist in the Third World from Paul
Simon's *Graceland* album, with its wide range of South African musicians and styles. The more experienced or widely
travelled may remember the ground-breaking records by
Simon "Mahlathini" Nkabinde in the mid-sixties, where, for
the first time, traditional melodies and rhythmic patterns
(including his famous "groaner" style of singing) were tran-
scribed for electric guitars and trap drums and given the name
mbaqanga or "township jive."

The comparatively vigorous economy of the Union of South
Africa has drawn workers from all over the southern quarter
of the continent, setting up a musical dialogue between tribes
and nations that results in the most cosmopolitan musical
society in all of Africa. Only Nigeria can boast a comparable
scene, thanks in part to the traditional West African *griot*

brotherhood—singer-poets who wander the land like bees cross-pollinating the various regional styles of the interior.

But in South Africa it is the people themselves who journey across regions and cultures to form the new musical landscape. Both the music and the musicians arise out of this diaspora, so it is natural that they should strike a chord with audiences of the industrialized world, many of whom are themselves involved in this kind of migration and whose enjoyment of African music is the product of the same kind of multicultural society.

PAUL SIMON

Although it is certainly not a pure expression of South African music, the first album the neophyte will want to consider is Paul Simon's *Graceland* (Warner Brothers 25447), as good an introduction as any to the varied sounds of the region. Simon's airy tenor is well-suited to township jive, and the lilting tunes are among the most refreshing and accessible of his long career.

As a songwriter, Simon has usually required an outside musical concern to keep his work from getting too self-conscious, too over-reliant on craft, too closed off from the needs, or even the understanding, of his listeners. *Graceland* achieves the desired openness with ease, the melodies powering the lyrics and not the other way around, the singing and playing always fresh and interesting thanks to a canny blending of South African and American musicians, all of whom offer distinctive musical statements, in contrast to the faceless New York triple-scalers who so often play on Simon's records.

Some will find *Graceland* a bit too all-over-the-map stylistically, especially with the extraneous *zydeco* and accordion-rock cuts at the end. It does indeed suffer from the curse of the encyclopaedia, but as the first attempt to put folk-poetry songwriting into an international context it is an admirable piece of work and provocative, stimulating entertainment.

LADYSMITH BLACK MAMBAZO

The South African group that probably benefitted most from their exposure on *Graceland* was the Zulu men's choir Ladysmith Black Mambazo ("Ladysmith" is the hometown of leader Joseph Shabalala and "mambazo" means "axe"). Records of unaccompanied choral hymn singing have long been popular with South African blacks, and by the time of *Graceland* the black axe from Ladysmith had been the most popular gospel choir in the country for a decade or more. With their subsequent worldwide success has come some inevitable dilution of style. Their 1990 album, *Two Worlds, One Heart* (Warner Brothers 26125-2), pairs them with a full band on some tracks, and most of the songs they sing now—on record, on "Sesame Street," or for soft-drink commercials—are secular in nature.

But the group's warm, baritone-heavy sound and Shabalala's engaging singing could make telephone listings sound cheery. And of the more than two dozen albums they had released in South Africa by the time they appeared on *Graceland,* a good half-dozen or so have been released in this country by Shanachie Records. One of the best of these, and the best place to start with this group, is *Classic Tracks* (Shanachie CD 43074). This retrospective features the best from those pre-*Graceland* albums.

Classic Tracks features less of the comic call-and-response that Ladysmith engages in nowadays, but the soaring harmonies are the same and, even though the lyrics are all in Zulu, Shabalala remains a sweet, sunny presence. The focus here is on the strong melodies of Shabalala's compositions, treating his mellifluous vocals more as a part of the ensemble than as its leader.

MAHLATHINI AND THE MOHATELLA QUEENS

The fifty-one-year-old Simon "Mahlathini" Nkabinde (aka "the

Lion of Soweto") is widely credited with having invented the *mbaqanga* style of South African dance-pop, first combining traditional Zulu melodies for voice and accordion with electric guitars and trap drums in 1965. With the three Mohatella Queens, he has developed a balanced, varied sound, the women's vocal harmonies punctuated by his impossibly deep bass-falsetto roars, suggesting a hitherto unimaginable pairing of the Andrews Sisters and Howlin' Wolf. Mahlathini has been a seminal force in South African music from the sixties, through a fallow period when African music was diluted by Westernized pop, and into its explosion of worldwide popularity in recent years.

Most songs feature the Mohatella Queens' plangent three-part singing interspersed with Mahlathini's wide vocabulary of groans, shouts, and exclamations, using a bass-falsetto reminiscent of American folk-blues singers like Blind Willie Johnson and often displaying an eerie similarity to the redoubtable sixties art-rocker Captain Beefheart.

A typical number starts with a hopping, stuttering riff from the Makgona Tsohle Band ("the Band That Knows Everything"). The three women then begin to sing, in either Zulu or Sotho. The song might be about the eternal heritage of black Africa ("Ifa Laphakade"), or a village's most beautiful young girl ("Ntombi Yakwa Nkabinde"), or the importance of getting an education ("Thuto Ke Senotlolo"). The Mohatella Queens, who started as dancers with Mahlathini in the early days, have become compelling singers. But just when the groove is at its hottest and you feel it can go no higher, Mahlathini (whose part is traditionally called "the groaner" or "the goat voice") steps in and lets out a roar that splits your skull.

In concert all four are energetic, nonstop dancers, but their dancing is less a choreographed show than it is an ongoing, improvised celebration of the music. Dances are taken like instrumental solos by each of the four, and, as each in turn demonstrates their best steps, the show takes on the competitive edge of a "cutting session" among jazz musicians.

Mahlathini and the Mohatella Queens. *Courtesy Shanachie Records*

But for all Mahlathini's willingness to share the spotlight, his is obviously the music's commanding intelligence, and as the rhythmic dynamism of his singing leads the band into one supple groove after another, one is reminded of great improvisors like Bix Beiderbecke, whose manifest sense of swing could carry even the most lead-footed accompanists to glory.

Both Mahlathini and the Mohatella Queens have albums released under their own names along with their joint projects, and the various products are more or less indistinguishable from each other, at least to the outsider. But Mahlathini has also released *You're Telling Tales* (Shanachie CD 43069) with Amaswazi Emvelo, a group of traditional singers from the Swazi tribe recruited by producer West Nkosi to add a different flavor to the often Zulu-dominated *mbaqanga* sound. The result is a distinctive and unusual work that stands quite alone among recent African releases. To the soulful singing and energetic dance rhythms are added guitars in open tunings that will sound familiar to devotees of the Mississippi blues.

The Lion Roars (Shanachie CD 43081) is a reissue of key tracks by Mahlathini and the Queens, some of which have been released in this country on compilations. It is a balanced and consistent work that contains several songs that are now favorites in concert. The Mohatella Queens' *Marriage Is a Problem* (Shanachie CD 43080) contains some wry observations that will amuse even those who cannot speak Zulu.

JOHNNY CLEGG, SAVUKA, AND JULUKA

Another South African to receive wide notice in the United States is the white, university-educated anthropologist Johnny Clegg and his multiracial band Savuka. Clegg created quite a stir with the debut album of his first group, Juluka, by appearing on the cover in full Zulu ceremonial dress standing beside his Zulu partner, Sipho Mchunu. Ever since, Clegg has incorporated his wide research into Zulu folkways into his act, particularly some spectacular tribal dancing.

From the beginning, Clegg's music, and his life, has been about assimilation, a white progressive's accommodation to the oncoming black majority. Clegg is an honorary member of the Zulu nation, participating fully in all of its rituals, including the Zulu "second marriage," where husband and wife renew their wedding vows after the birth of their first child. At this ceremony, the only concession to Western sensibilities was a special dispensation allowing Mrs. Clegg to wear a tank top while performing the ritual dances.

When Mchunu bought a farm and retired, Clegg formed Savuka, with whom he has toured the world and released several albums. Juluka was in many ways the more interesting of the two groups, with deeper roots in both Celtic and Zulu folk, while Savuka plays a more formularized African dance-pop. Savuka's *Cruel, Crazy, Beautiful World* (Capitol C11H 93446) has plenty of satisfying moments, but the harder-to-find *Best of Juluka* (Rhythm Safari CDL 57138) creates a fascinating synthesis of African and European styles, Zulu drumming and the "groaner" vocal style of *mbaqanga* mixing with Gaelic tunefulness in tightly crafted songs of love, worship, and adventure.

THOMAS MAPFUMO AND THE MUSIC OF ZIMBABWE

Zimbabwean music is similar to that of black South Africa, not surprising considering the two countries' close proximity and common tribal heritage. But Zimbabwean pop music is simpler, almost stark, and comes more directly from traditional sources than does South African township jive. It still includes traditional instruments like the *hosho* (shaker) and *mbira* (thumb-piano). The musicians are perhaps less worldly-wise than their South African counterparts, but their music is every bit as charming. Songs tend to avoid boy-meets-girl platitudes and deal instead with social problems, tribal customs, and cautionary tales. It is refreshing, even in translation, to hear songs that warn children against playing with matches, or say, "Thanks again to those who fought for our liberation."

Thomas Mapfumo, whose place in Zimbabwe is analogous to that of Mahlathini in South Africa, began in music by transposing *mbira* lines to electric guitar and *hosho* patterns to the cymbals. Through the *chimurenga* ("struggle" in the Shona language) that changed the country from the white-run oligarchy known as Rhodesia to the majority-rule state of Zimbabwe, Mapfumo's music was in many ways the seminal propaganda force of the progressive movement. In a country where many are illiterate, popular music often assumes the function of newspapers or magazines; Mapfumo's songs were often banned from government radio, which apparently had no effect on their popularity.

Mapfumo's *The Chimurenga Singles* (Shanachie CD 43066) is the best document of that period of his work, a time spent recording in makeshift studios deep in the bush and distributing the records through an informal network of dancehalls and parties. The sound is not particularly glossy, as one might expect, and one occasionally wonders how music this light and bouncy could be seen as a threat by the ruling party, but in closer listening the intensity is there in Mapfumo's singing. This is a valuable document.

A more recent release, with considerably better production values, is *Corruption* (Mango CCD 9848). Despite the lack of a full-scale insurrection to inspire him, Mapfumo sings here with riveting intensity over chiming, burbling tracks recorded in a state-of-the-art studio in Zimbabwe's capital city of Harare. The title cut, a biting attack on government ministers who abuse the public trust, is sung in English, but the rest of the songs are in Shona, with texts welcoming rebel fighters back from the bush or chiding indifferent husbands who spend all of their money on prostitutes.

One of my favorite Zimbabwean recordings is *Machanic Manyeruke and the Puritans* (Flying Fish FF 70553). The album notes are not very complete, but this Shona-speaking gospel quartet sounds like they spend most of their time evangelizing on Harare street corners. The principal instrument is Manyeruke's electric guitar, strummed quickly but with amazing accuracy behind his high, urgent singing (at times echoing Paul Simon's light, vibratoless vocal attack). Manyeruke is accompanied by an uncredited electric organist, who appears to be playing only the bass notes much of the time, and two uncredited female singers in a call-and-response style chorus.

Machanic Manyeruke. *Courtesy Flying Fish Records*

The quality of the emotion sets this release apart. The singers' evident sincerity and utter lack of affectation are very winning, and the rhythms, while not as driving as those of a full band, are solid enough to put a lift in anyone's step. This is my favorite album to listen to while washing the dishes.

One of the best-known Zimbabwean groups, especially in Europe, is the Bhundu Boys, formed just after independence in 1980. Their album, *Pamberi!* (Mango CCD 9858), is a subtle and deeply felt work of pop music, with the most advanced production values yet to come out of Harare. There is some question as to whether the squeaky-clean recording takes the music one step away from the necessary grit of good African music, but the group's sophistication can be explained at least partially by their long stays in England.

Pamberi! does contain some moments of traditional *mbira* music, with thumb-piano and shakers, but they seem to be inserted mostly for contrast. Still, most of the guitar parts are played in the fingerpicking Zimbabwean style and there can be no doubt that the group draws on the roots of *mbira* to produce the flower they have created.

Other worthwhile Zimbabwean artists are Stella Chiwese, whose *Ambaya* (Shanachie CD 65006) showcases her sweet singing and deft arranging touch, and the Four Brothers, an unrelated quartet boasting the hottest guitar playing outside of the West African *soukous* camp. Their *Makorokoto* (Flying Fish/Atomic Theory ATD 1106) has met with considerable success in this country. A more folkloric take on the music of the Shona tribe is found in the work of Dumisani "Dumi" Maraire, whose *Chaminuka: Music of Zimbabwe* (Music of the World CDT 208) draws on the traditional thumb-piano and keening vocals.

TONY BIRD

Another white singer-songwriter in the African tradition, and one who was performing in exile long before the world had ever heard of Johnny Clegg, is Tony Bird, who was born and raised in Malawi. Built around acoustic guitar, Bird's music is

Tony Bird. *Courtesy Philo Records*

utterly charming, a deceptively simple and completely unique blend of African folk styles from English, Boer, and Zulu traditions alike, with quavering voice over guitar strings snapped like a thumb-piano, the mysterious rhythm of the veldt informing every phrase.

After some time spent travelling the world in the merchant marine, Bird developed enough of a European reputation that the South African government refused to let him return home, so he settled in New York. Needless to say, nobody in the American or English music business ever quite knew what to do with him, despite two fine LPs for Columbia in the late 1970s. Then Bird's longtime partner, the saxophonist and pennywhistler Morris Goldberg, became an important part of the *Graceland* album and subsequent Paul Simon tours.

Goldberg used his new-found clout to produce a fine album of Bird's best songs, *Sorry Africa* (Philo CDPH 1135). Some of these numbers have been part of Bird's set for years—like "Zambezi-Zimbabwe," a hymn to the liberation of Rhodesia, and "Mango Time," here given the full *mbaqanga* treatment with an all-star band of Paul Simon and Hugh Masakela sidemen. The new songs tend to be quieter, almost delicate, but unmistakably the work of a unique and distinctive musical personality.

COMPILATIONS

Before *Graceland,* the music of Southern Africa, like so many world styles, was chiefly represented in this country through compilation albums, and several of these anthologies remain solid, entertaining packages that give an overview of various regional scenes. These albums also avoid some of the inevitable monochrome effect of one-artist albums.

Perhaps the best-known of these compilations is *The Indestructible Beat of Soweto* (Shanachie CD 43033), a package so beloved among world-music fans that the title has been used by other record labels, as on *Freedom Fire: The Inde-*

structible Beat of Soweto Volume 3 (Virgin/Earthworks 91409-2), itself a laudable package that includes some great Mahlathini tracks. The Shanachie package is pure, bare-bones township jive, with no concessions to modern pop-music trends, one of the most honest and human albums ever made.

Homeland: A Collection of Black South African Music (Rounder CD 11549) was well on its way to winning the 1988 Grammy Award for Best Contemporary Folk Performance when it was swamped by the Tracy Chapman juggernaut. A sequel, *Homeland 2* (Rounder CD 5028), is every bit as varied, dynamic, and entertaining as its predecessor. These packages range from funky dance music to devotional songs, with a strong emphasis on the guitar-and-voice roots of the music.

To illustrate just how down-home some of this is, the liner notes to *Homeland 2* include this story: One of the performers on *Homeland 2* simply appeared at a recording studio one day with his accordion and a drummer, laid down ten tracks without telling anyone his name, and left saying he would return shortly to complete the songs. Two years passed and not a word was heard from him. The producer liked the tracks so much that he finished them himself and released it under the name Mohahlehi—"the lost one"—asking radio announcers to appeal publicly for the singer to contact him. The album was a major success but to date the singer has still not been found. His royalties, deposited for him in a Johannesburg bank, continue to mount.

These four compilations are probably the best albums for those who liked *Graceland* and want to hear more of the same without having to review the music of an entire continent. Not only are these some of the recordings that inspired Paul Simon, but they include cuts by the Boyoyo Boys, who appear on *Graceland* and who were the first South African group Simon heard on the famous unmarked cassette, given Simon by a friend, that started his African pilgrimage.

Outside of Ladysmith Black Mambazo, few of South Africa's many great black choirs have released complete albums in this country, but there are some excellent collections to be had. Most of these have yet to make the transition to compact disc, but there is one that is an excellent source both of great music and historical perspective: *Mbube Roots: Zulu Choral Music from South Africa, 1930s–1960s* (Rounder CD 5025).

Zimbabwean pop music is well documented on a pair of compilations: *Zimbabwe Frontline* (Virgin/Earthworks 91001-2) and *Spirit of the Eagle: Zimbabwe Frontline Volume 2* (Virgin/Earthworks 91410-2). The first *Zimbabwe Frontline* package features Thomas Mapfumo and others in strongly political performances inspired by the struggle for majority rule. The second volume is more a peacetime affair, again with Mapfumo dominating, and with some ringing, guitar-driven tracks by the Four Brothers.

OTHER SOUTHERN AFRICAN SOUNDS

Other countries in Southern Africa have their own distinctive popular musics. But the economies of the so-called "frontline states" have been severely weakened by decades of unrest along their borders with South Africa, and many of their best musicians have been forced to live and work in Europe or North America, with the inevitable dilution of style.

Mozambique's Eyuphuro works out of Toronto mostly, using what expatriate musicians he can find as accompanists. His CD *Mama Mosambiki* (Virgin/RealWorld 91347-2) is an airy acoustic meditation, the vocals floating over gut-stringed guitars and the lighter percussion instruments. Eyuphuro is a charming singer, and his songs show a real grasp of craft, but one wishes he and his compatriots were able to return more often to the unalloyed roots of their music, seemingly inaccessible in a wasteland of war and poverty.

DISCOGRAPHY

Paul Simon: *Graceland* (Warner Brothers 25447)

Ladysmith Black Mambazo: *Two Worlds, One Heart* (Warner Brothers 26125-2) and **Classic Tracks (Shanachie CD 43074)

Mahlathini with Amaswazi Emvelo: *You're Telling Tales* (Shanachie CD 43069)

**Mahlathini with the Mohatella Queens: *The Lion Roars* (Shanachie CD 43081)

The Mohatella Queens: *Marriage Is a Problem* (Shanachie CD 43080)

Johnny Clegg and Savuka: *Cruel, Crazy, Beautiful World* (Capitol C11H 93446)

**Best of Juluka (Rhythm Safari CDL 57138)

Thomas Mapfumo: *The Chimurenga Singles* (Shanachie CD 43066) and *Corruption* (Mango CCD 9848)

***Machanic Manyeruke and the Puritans* (Flying Fish FF 70553)

The Bhundu Boys: *Pamberi!* (Mango CCD 9858)

Stella Chiwese: *Ambaya* (Shanachie CD 65006)

The Four Brothers: *Makorokoto* (Flying Fish/Atomic Theory ATD 1106)

Dumisani "Dumi" Maraire: *Chaminuka: Music of Zimbabwe* (Music of the World CDT 208)

Tony Bird: *Sorry Africa* (Philo CDPH 1135)

***The Indestructible Beat of Soweto* (Shanachie CD 43033)

***Freedom Fire: The Indestructible Beat of Soweto Volume 3* (Virgin/Earthworks 91409-2)

Homeland: A Collection of Black South African Music (Rounder CD 11549); *Homeland 2* (Rounder CD 5028)

Mbube Roots: Zulu Choral Music from South Africa, 1930s–1960s (Rounder CD 5025)

Zimbabwe Frontline (Virgin/Earthworks 91001-2)

Spirit of the Eagle: Zimbabwe Frontline Volume 2 (Virgin/Earthworks 91410-2)

Eyuphuro: *Mama Mosambiki* (Virgin/RealWorld 91347-2)

**Highly recommended

2

〰〰〰〰〰〰〰〰〰〰〰〰〰〰〰〰

WESTERN AFRICA

DAVE VAN RONK CALLS the dance-pop of Western Africa "this decade's equivalent to Coors Beer in the sixties. In those days you drank Coors to subtly indicate that you had been to Aspen. Nowadays you listen to Loketo to subtly indicate you've been to Paris."

It is true that in the thriving West African dance-pop scene Paris has become as much of a nerve center as Kinshasa, Lagos, or Dakar. French audiences have always responded warmly to the music of their former colonies, be it Cajun, Polynesian, or *soukous*. But the flashy, high-powered music that fills the discos and dance clubs of Paris is only part of the story of this extraordinarily diverse region. At one extreme you can hear penniless travelling bards called *griots* ("Jali" in the Mandingo language) sing traditional songs of the Mandingo diaspora, and at another extreme tribal kings, further enriched by oil revenues, dance to huge orchestras made up of their titled retainers.

FELA

The Nigerian bandleader, polemicist, and saxophone player Fela Anikulapo Kuti became an international symbol of musical dissent, comparable to the late Bob Marley, when the Nigerian government jailed him in 1984 on questionable charges of currency smuggling. Eighteen months in jail did nothing to tone down his barbed criticisms of Nigerian and world leaders and, although he is now allowed to tour the world freely with his gigantic band, Egypt 80, concerts in his home country are still often broken up by soldiers.

Fela Anikulapo Kuti. *Courtesy Shanachie Records*

Fela has been making his own brand of rambling, polyrhythmic African funk since the early seventies. In his songs the grooves seem to come from out of nowhere, with percussion, electric piano, horn, and guitar lines layering in seemingly at random. A single song will roll through dozens of changes—on record for up to twenty-five minutes and in concert for as much as three hours—while Fela sings, sometimes in an indecipherable patois and sometimes with biting clarity, of the social and political ills besetting the world. It can be the most hypnotic and uncompromisingly rooted music you have ever heard.

Fela's political pronouncements carry an even greater authority because they are untainted by racism. The governments of Nigeria, South Africa, the United States, and Europe are attacked with equal force—and none are given any quarter. *Beasts of No Nation* (Shanachie CD 43070) avoids, however, the note of arrogant self-indulgence that has marred some of Fela's albums. (It's hard to be humble when you have twenty-seven wives.) With its borderline-dissonant harmonies and gossamer-light funk rhythms, it is simply the most distinctive, unusual, and listenable political music being made today.

O.D.O.O. / Overtake Don Overtake Overtake (Shanachie CD 43078) also makes a powerful statement. Fela has always been as much a public speaker as a singer, and here his declamatory vocals are wedded to a subject near to his heart— his mother, who died of injuries she received when Nigerian troops attacked Fela's compound, burned his recording studio, and threw her out of an upstairs window. It is one thing for rich, privileged Anglo-American pop musicians to embrace recycling and Martin Luther King, quite another for a victim of genuine oppression to voice his anger with this much truth and soul.

Standouts among Fela's many other releases are *The Best of Fela, Volumes 1 & 2* (Oceana/Celluloid 4104-2Q) and *Live with Ginger Baker* (Celluloid CELCD 6134). And recently the early-eighties recordings that led to his arrest have been reissued in this country under the title *Original Sufferhead* (Shanachie CD 44010).

SOUKOUS

From Zaire, Loketo ("Hips") is perhaps the best of several Paris-based groups that play *soukous* ("shake") music, a powerful amalgam of melodic guitars, polyrhythmic drumming,

Loketo. *Courtesy Shanachie Records*

and sweet vocal melodies. The group is led by the masterful guitarist Diblo Dibala, whose ringing chromatic lead figures anchor the arrangements. The two guitars, bass, and trap drums are joined by singers Jean Baron and Aurlus Mabele, who is also the group's cofounder and frontman.

Soukous bears an uncanny resemblance to the *compas-direct* style of Haitian groups like Tabou Combo. That the Lingala patois of the *soukous* bands sounds a lot like Haiti's Creole French is perhaps the least of the similarities. Diblo's chiming guitar tone sounds very much like that of Tabou Combo's Elysée Pyronneau, and their chromaticism is also much the same. There is plenty of similarity in the speedy, percolating rhythms of the two musics, perhaps because Haitian music is the least Americanized of Caribbean styles, although Tabou Combo will quote from other genres in ways that Loketo does not.

In concert, Mabele and Loketo's two female dancers often pull men and women out of the audience, egging them on with ever-more-pelvic gestures and movements and refusing to be topped no matter how frenzied the response. Although patrons line up to take turns bumping and grinding with the dancers onstage, the erotic content of Loketo's music is decidedly nonthreatening and inclusive. They aim for release, not surrender. *Soukous Trouble* (Shanachie CD 64025) and *Super Soukous* (Shanachie CD 64016) both give Diblo plenty of room to shine, and he makes the most of it, crafting one brilliant circular figure after another over the playful rhythms of drummer Mack Macaire and percussionist Komba.

Diblo Dibala began his career with the most popular worldwide star of *soukous*, Kanda Bongo Man. Kanda's 1991 release, *Zing Zong* (Hannibal HNCD 1366), is his best yet, in many ways outshining even Loketo. Where Loketo is a more-or-less cooperative venture, with some of the inevitable dilu-

Kanda Bongo Man. *Courtesy Hannibal/Rykodisc*

tion of focus that that implies, Kanda Bongo Man—as lead singer, producer, arranger, and principal songwriter—is the undisputed leader of his group. This unity of vision results in an album of rare purity, with few concessions to European and American tastes (there are no synthesizers, for instance). The lead guitar player on *Zing Zong* is Nene Tchakou and he ably fills Diblo's giant shoes.

Diblo himself is featured on Kanda Bongo Man's previous U.S. release *Kwassa Kwassa* (Hannibal HNCD 1337). The "kwassa kwassa" of the title is the befuddled "Quoi ça!" of a French-speaking driver lost in the sprawling neighborhoods of Kinshasa. "What's that!" he cries at each new landmark. It has since become a popular chant on dance floors across Europe. At first it may be hard for some ears to distinguish one song from another on *Kwassa Kwassa,* but anyone will notice the brilliant twin-guitar attack of Diblo and Ringo Star (no, not *that* Ringo Starr).

TSHALA MUANA

A gentler and more lyrical take on *soukous* is provided by Tshala Muana, one of a growing number of female *soukous* stars. Her album *Soukous Siren* (Shanachie CD 64031) deliberately holds back the pounding drive of most male-dominated groups in favor of more moderate tempos and beautiful melodies.

That is not to say that *Soukous Siren* is at all pudgy or lethargic. It's just that the rhythms seem to come out of the melodies instead of being imposed on them. *Soukous Siren* is full of movement and life, quite danceable for those whose metabolisms are not on full-tilt overdrive, and behind Muana's effortless singing the music seems to sway. Unlike many female stars in African music, she is directly involved in all facets of her music, coproducing the album and writing most of the material. As a result, *Soukous Siren* is a focused and consistent piece of work. Boasting well-written songs as opposed to riffs, it is one of the most listenable and pleasurable of recent *soukous* releases and an album I come back to again and again.

TABU LEY ROCHEREAU AND M'BILIA BEL

Rochereau is the most popular singer in Zaire, although ironically this serves to limit his American audience. There are two reasons for this. First, he has released so many albums in Africa and Europe that they tend to be rereleased here in large batches, and the predictable lack of consistency in the product (often recorded over widely varying periods of time) makes those who don't get the good stuff wonder what all the fuss is about. Then there is the ongoing question of what to call him. In his earliest LP releases, he was billed as just "Tabu Ley," and one assumed his first name was "Tabu" and his last name "Ley." Now it seems he has three names, and some releases refer to him simply as "Rochereau" and some as "Tabu Ley Rochereau." There is at least one album credited to "Rochereau" whose title is *Tabu Ley*!

The CD that solves all these problems for the American consumer is *Franco and Rochereau: Omona Wapi* (Shanachie CD 43024). This guitar-heavy duet album with fellow-Zairean Franco avoids the dickety-dickety horn sound of some of Rochereau's other *soukous* offerings, giving plenty of room to his high, supple voice, piquantly contrasted with Franco's earthier, more rhythmic tones. No song clocks in at less than seven minutes, so the grooves build up a good head of steam, and the melodies are bright and pretty. This is a listenable, relaxing record with steady rhythms and an affectingly naive charm.

Another rewarding album by Rochereau, credited to "Tabu Ley and his Africa International Orchestra," is *Babeti Soukous* (Virgin/RealWorld 91302-2). This date finds him in front of a large band with a lot of horns, blasting away in the hard-charging style that made him famous. This is perhaps the best of Rochereau's pure dance music currently available in the United States. The material is consistently tuneful and the production values, courtesy of Peter Gabriel's RealWorld label, are first-rate.

M'bilia Bel is a protégé of Rochereau's who has gone on to a prominent solo career. Like Tshala Muana, and most other female singers in *soukous,* she started as a dancer, working in Rochereau's chorus until she was given a featured singing role on his album *Tabu Ley* (Shanachie CD 43017), perhaps the most harmonically advanced of his albums available here and a dynamic, exciting piece of work. Rochereau returns the favor on Bel's first album, *Bameli Soy* (Shanachie CD 43025), and the subtle contrast between the two voices—both of them high and sweet but the one urgent and forceful, the other gently pliant—adds a distinctive flavor to music that in lesser hands can be flashy and shallow.

LES TÊTES BRULÉES

As if in reaction to the glitz of other West African groups, the

Les Têtes Brulées. *Courtesy Shanachie Records*

outrageous high-energy quintet Les Têtes Brulées (pronounced "lay TET broo-LAY," literally "the Hot Heads") call their music "Bikutski rock" after the traditional rhythm of the Cameroonian rainforest, but it would not be going too far to call them Afro-punk.

The group was founded in 1986 by the *Cameroon Tribune*'s music critic Jean-Marie Ahanda as a reaction against the flashy, sophisticated music that had dominated local airwaves for more than a decade. Unlike the more polished stars of Cameroon, with their large horn sections and legions of back-up singers, Les Têtes Brulées are a rough-edged little group whose five members all dance, sing, and play—all at the same time. And instead of the extravagant clothes of the stars, the group wears outlandish rags, bizarre body paint, and day-glo backpacks that symbolize the rural peasant who can carry everything he owns on his back.

The music on *Hot Heads* (Shanachie CD 64030) is chattering and guitar-driven, with a crazy edge not found elsewhere in African music. Tracks can be preceded by hysterical laughter, or dissolve into free-form cadences that at their outer limits sound almost like Captain Beefheart. With rhythms relentlessly up and in your face, the hottest aerobic workout imaginable, *Hot Heads* explodes the clichés of slick, sweet Afro-pop.

JUJU MUSIC

The first West African style to grab the attention of North American listeners was the *juju* music of Nigeria's Yoruba tribe, in an early-eighties invasion led by King Sunny Ade (pronounced "ah-DAY"). Ade became quite a media star for a while, his picture in everything from "downtown" tabloid papers to ladies' fashion magazines. His music, its billowing polyryhtms the work of a half-dozen or more drummers, was a welcome relief from the stripped-down, derivative patterns of the new-wave pop music dominating that time.

Juju combines the traditional talking-drum patterns of the jungle with soft, sugary male singing and electric and slide guitars. In the hands of King Sunny Ade and the other principal figure in the music, Chief Commander Ebenezer Obey (Yoruba society is strictly monarchical and both men are the scions of titled families), the sound is at the same time impossibly light and impossibly hard-driving.

To Western ears this seems a paradox. But the fact is that *juju* is dance music in a relentless whisper. The rhythms are so sweeping, and the harmonic overlay so seductive (especially when combined in the recording studio with glistening Jamaican-style "dub" effects), that you will wonder what you have been dancing to, and where the last three hours have gone. The restraint with which the musicians play gives their

Chief Commander Ebenezer Obey. *Courtesy Shanachie Records*

music a tremendous power, a lesson that could be well-learned by English and American rock bands.

The album that started it all in this country is King Sunny Ade's *Juju Music* (Mango CCD 9712), and it remains a definitive statement of the form. Since then, Ade and Obey have traded albums the way the Beatles and the Rolling Stones used to do. At one point they even put out back-to-back live albums on the same record label: King Sunny Ade and his African Beats *Live Live Juju* (Rykodisc RCD 10047) and Chief Commander Ebenezer Obey and his Inter-Reformers Band *Get Yer Jujus Out* (Rykodisc RCD 20111).

Both bands feature roughly the same lineup and the two leaders have similar-sounding voices. But, generally speaking, Obey is the more traditional of the two, with less emphasis on studio effects and more on guitar playing, especially in the retrospective *Juju Jubilee* (Shanachie CD 43031), featuring plenty of hot steel-guitar licks. Ade has come to prefer a slightly harder edge in recent studio recordings, and takes more chances generally. His latest album, *Aura* (Mango CCD 9824), even features a smoking chromatic-harmonica solo from Stevie Wonder. Any of these five albums will shake you.

OLATUNJI

The same kind of Yoruba drumming one hears in *juju* is expanded and given a more biting attack by the master percussionist Babatunde Olatunji. Olatunji, whose international recording career has thrived for thirty years, is heard at his best on two albums produced by Grateful Dead drummer Mickey Hart—part of Hart's monumental series of ethnic and field recordings called "The World." On *Drums of Passion: The Invocation* (Rykodisc RCD 10102) and *Drums of Passion: The Beat* (Rykodisc RCD 10107), Hart himself, the legendary Brazilian drummer Airto Moreira, and guitarist Carlos Santana are part of a twenty-three-piece band, twelve members of which play some sort of drum.

Recorded to the highest standards of audio technology, these tracks are not merely milling all-star jam sessions but focused, intent expressions of Olatunji's muse. That they give talented rock-music players like Santana a new context to play in is a bonus; Santana, for one, responds with some of the most fiercely joyful playing of his career. The drum grooves are furious but never overstated, the singers chanting unison melodies over them in a near-trance. This is the rare transcultural fusion that results in true magic.

Much of Olatunji's back catalogue remains out of print in this country, although the original *Drums of Passion* (Columbia CK 8210)—a staple of black-nationalist dance companies for generations—has been reissued. And Olatunji appears from time to time on other "The World" CDs, including Mickey Hart's new-age inflected *At the Edge* (Rykodisc RCD 10124).

SALIF KEITA

Another West African artist able to experiment within traditional forms without losing his music's distinctive feel is the brilliant Malian singer Salif Keita. In the 1987 release *Soro* (Mango CCD 9808), Keita and producer Ibrahima Sylla bring production values worthy of a big-budget pop album to a firmly-rooted, ecstatic vocal style.

Mali is landlocked, its northern reaches extending into the Sahara Desert, so there is a strongly Islamic cast to Keita's singing. But the arrangements here, whether they feature a big band with lots of horns or smaller guitar-and-keyboard settings, draw more on the Gold Coast. *Soro* was recorded in Paris, and the European influence is strong not so much in the elements Keita and Sylla use as in the way they use them. Keita's sense of dynamics is unparalleled in African music and his two arrangers, Jean-Phillipe Rikyel and François Breant, know how to exploit it well. Their combination of influences is perfectly seamless.

But despite the sympathetic backing, it is Keita's songs and his singing of them that sells this package in the end. Although the Senegalese singer Youssou N'Dour has a higher profile in the world (thanks in part to his association with the British pop singer Peter Gabriel), Keita's is the most compelling voice to come out of West Africa, an instrument with technical assurance and emotional commitment second to none. I have been told that by the time this volume is published there should be a new recording available from Salif Keita, as yet untitled, and I am sure it will also be well worth hearing.

Ali Farka Toure. *Photo by Dave Peabody, courtesy Shanachie Records*

ALI FARKA TOURE

Another fine artist from Mali is the expert guitarist and spell-binding singer Ali Farka Toure, who creates one of the most distinctive syntheses yet to come out of Africa. In the past, all musicians in Mali came from a few families, whose low social status reinforced the rigid traditions in which the music continued. Ali Farka Toure was not born into one of these families, thus his love of music—especially records by American singers like John Lee Hooker, Albert King, and Otis Redding—led him into a completely original style.

On both *African Blues* (Shanachie CD 65002) and *Ali Farka Toure* (Mango CCD 9826) he can sound for all the world like a classic Mississippi Delta bluesman, in the intensity of his singing and the way his electric guitar embraces the rhythms and harmonies of the form. Then, just as you expect to hear Charley Patton's voice, he begins to sing the ancient *griot* songs of the savannah. It results in a beautiful confusion.

THE GRIOTS

The *griot* brotherhood are the wandering bards of the Mandingo tribe throughout Mali, Gambia, Guinea, and Senegal. "Griot" is French—in Mandingo, the word is "Jali." Their principal instrument is the *kora,* the chiming twenty-one-string lyre of sub-Saharan Africa. Jali Musa Jawara is originally from Guinea and now lives in Ivory Coast, where his album *Yasimika* (Hannibal HNCD 1355) was recorded in 1983. *Yasimika* combines the *kora* with two gut-string guitars, a marimba-like instrument called the *balafon,* and a three-voice female chorus in a haunting, ethereal wash of pure sound.

This is not modern electronic dance-pop. It is an arranged and updated version of the traditional acoustic music of the savannah region south of the western Sahara. The rhythm is not so much a beat as a pulse, but despite its subtlety the music is quietly exhilarating, with an eerie, timeless quality, the sensuality of the women's voices playing against the bell-like harmonics of the *kora* and the gentle rhythms of the guitars.

Also playing the folk music of the Mandingo diaspora is Alhaji Bai Konte, who has been a favorite of American folk festival audiences for several years, especially celebrated by Taj Mahal. His *Kora Music of Gambia* (Rounder CD 5001) comes closest to being an accurate picture of his homeland's musical landscape.

Another virtuoso of the *kora* is Foday Musa Suso, who has also cultivated an American reputation since the mid-seventies. Suso, however, is far from traditional in his outlook. Although his album *The Dreamtime* (CMP CD 3001) puts his original songs in a more-or-less traditional context, he is better-known for ground-breaking stylistic fusions like his work with avant-funk bassist Bill Laswell in the group Mandingo. Mandingo's *New World Power* (Axiom 539876-2) is a churning cauldron of electronic drums, studio effects, and synthesizers,

Mandingo Griot Society. *Courtesy Flying Fish Records*

with the *kora* floating effortlessly on top of the mix and Suso's declaiming vocals pushing the rhythms along.

But to my ears the most interesting of Suso's fusion attempts is one of his first, the recently re-issued *Mandingo Griot Society* (Flying Fish FF 70076). In this 1978 session, the percussion effects are all made by real instruments—trap drums, *tablas,* congas, timbales, bongos, shakers, bells, et al.—and they give the *kora* a strikingly *particular* setting, free of today's music-in-a-box samplings. The trumpet playing of world-jazz legend Don Cherry meshes perfectly with the acoustic funk put down by Suso and his three, one assumes from their names, American sidemen. *Mandingo Griot Society* works as both small-group acoustic jazz and as a subtle and nonintrusive change rung on *griot* tradition.

DISCOGRAPHY

Fela: *******Beasts of No Nation*** (Shanachie CD 43070); *O.D.O.O./Overtake Don Overtake Overtake* (Shanachie CD 43078); *The Best of Fela, Volumes 1 & 2* (Oceana/Celluloid 4104-2Q); *Live with Ginger Baker* (Celluloid CELCD 6134); and *Original Sufferhead* (Shanachie CD 44010)

Loketo: *Soukous Trouble* (Shanachie CD 64025) and *Super Soukous* (Shanachie CD 64016)

Kanda Bongo Man: *******Zing Zong*** (Hannibal HNCD 1366) and *Kwassa Kwassa* (Hannibal HNCD 1337)

**Tshala Muana: *Soukous Siren* (Shanachie CD 64031)

Franco and Rochereau: Omona Wapi (Shanachie CD 43024)

Tabu Ley and his Africa International Orchestra: *Babeti Soukous* (Virgin/RealWorld 91302-2)

Tabu Ley Rochereau: *Tabu Ley* (Shanachie CD 43017)

M'bilia Bel: *Bameli Soy* (Shanachie CD 43025)

Les Têtes Brulées: *Hot Heads* (Shanachie CD 64030)

King Sunny Ade and his African Beats: *******Juju Music*** (Mango CCD 9712); *Live Live Juju* (Rykodisc RCD 10047); and *Aura* (Mango CCD 9824)

Chief Commander Ebenezer Obey and his Inter-Reformers Band: *Get*

Yer Jujus Out (Rykodisc RCD 20111) and *Juju Jubilee (Shanachie CD 43031)

Olatunji: *Drums of Passion: The Invocation* (Rykodisc RCD 10102); **Drums of Passion: The Beat* (Rykodisc RCD 10107); and *Drums of Passion* (Columbia CK 8210)

Mickey Hart: *At the Edge* (Ryodisc RCD 10024)

**Salif Keita: *Soro* (Mango CCD 9808)

Ali Farka Toure: *African Blues* (Shanachie CD 65002) and *Ali Farka Toure* (Mango CCD 9826)

**Jali Musa Jawara: *Yasimika* (Hannibal HNCD 1355)

Alhaji Bai Konte: *Kora Music of Gambia* (Rounder CD 5001)

Foday Musa Suso: *The Dreamtime* (CMP CD 3001)

Mandingo: *New World Power* (Axiom 539876-2)

**Mandingo Griot Society* (Flying Fish FF 70076)

**Highly recommended

Samite. *Photo by Irene Young, courtesy Shanachie Records*

3

NORTHERN AND EASTERN AFRICA

THERE ARE A NUMBER of reasons why East African countries and the Arab world should be somewhat underrepresented, both here and in the *Schwann* catalogue. Not every region possesses the thriving recording industry that has so benefited West Africa, nor the kind of international political focus that makes the music of South African blacks so resonant. In many countries of Northern Africa and the Middle East, music, like the visual arts, is rigidly subsumed to the dictates of Islam and kept very much a private matter, not to be recorded or distributed widely. And many countries—some that come to mind are Uganda, Iraq, Libya, Ethiopia, and the "frontline" states on the border with Israel—are overwhelmed by war, famine, and political oppression, too buffeted by circumstance to concentrate on any cultural activity beyond staying alive.

But there are plenty of worthwhile, even valuable, releases from this part of the world, so if the reader will forgive me for grafting two regions together, we will review some great albums, without undue context-mongering.

RAI

The Algerian popular music known as *rai* started early in this century as transcriptions of the unaccompanied tribal songs of the interior for the saxophones and violins played by dance bands in the coastal cities. As this process continued, the influences of Algeria's Spanish, Moroccan, and French communities were felt (with a particular emphasis on *flamenco*). In recent years a new *rai* has emerged, called pop-*rai,* that incorporates Western rock and disco rhythms for synthesizers and drums. The large Algerian expatriate population in France has served as the springboard for the music's acceptance in Europe and North America.

Pop-*rai* grafts North African melodies onto synthesizer-driven dance-pop with lyrics sung in Arabic, the Moorish harmonies combining with Western dance pulses as if it were the most natural thing in the world. And although Arabic, with its aspirating consonants, takes a little getting used to as a vehicle for party sass, *rai* singers bring a passionate urgency to their performances that is contagious. There are about as many women as men singing *rai,* but some of the women do not allow their photographs to be displayed.

The producer Rachid Baba Achmed is the pre-eminent figure in the music and it was in his studio in the western town of Tlemcen that the music developed. The excellent compilation *Pop-Rai and Rachid Style* (Virgin/ Earthworks 91407-2) is a sampler of late-eighties hits from Rachid's sizeable stable of artists. True to the music's roots in unaccompanied solo singing, Rachid's standard technique is to record the vocalists alone first, adding instruments and synthesizers one at a time at his leisure, playing all the parts himself.

Perhaps the most popular Rachid-produced singer is Chaba Fadela, who released *Hana Hana* (Mango CCD 539856) with her husband Cheb Sahraoui in 1990. The titles Cheb ("young guy") and Chaba ("young woman") usually precede *rai* artists' names, a device also used by the English pop singer Boy George. Fadela is a forceful and dynamic singer, with a ululating vibrato that conveys great physical expressiveness. She was the biggest star in Algeria when she quit to marry Sahraoui a few years ago, and this is her triumphant comeback. Although Sahraoui is one of the greatest singers in *rai*, the fact is that Chaba Fadela came into the studio with something to prove, and prove it she does—cards, spades, and big casino.

Chaba Fadela. *Courtesy Mango Records*

A *rai* CD that features more musical instruments and fewer electronic effects is Cheb Mami's *Prince of Rai* (Shanachie CD 64013). This recording gives a better idea of the musical roots of *rai*: drummers, bass guitar, violin obligatto, and other instrumentalists forming an actual band behind the singer. The result is a sort of muzzein-rock, where the tracks may not have as much "happening" in them as Rachid's, but the interplay between the players gives the music a different sort of drive.

Mami is a fine singer. He's not in Chaba Fadela or Cheb Sahraoui's class, perhaps, but he understands the way these forms adapt to each other, the narrow harmonies and whiplash vocal attack of the desert melding with various dervish rhythms and the all-important touch of American funk. Chances are, if *rai* artists start touring North America, Mami would be a good one to catch because he is used to playing with a band already.

SAMITE, KENYA, AND BENGA MUSIC

One of the great "sleeper" albums of this survey comes from the Ugandan singer and flutist Samite, whose *Dance My Children Dance* (Shanachie CD 65003) is such a gentle and low-key set that it takes a few hearings before the listener realizes how sophisticated the music really is. Samite (pronounced "SAH-mee-tay") was taught the traditional Ugandan flute as a boy, "graduated" to the European flute, and then moved to Kenya where he built his reputation as that country's finest jazz flutist. He eventually returned to the music of his boyhood, establishing a large following in Nairobi before emigrating in 1987 to the United States, where he recorded this album.

Most folk-styled African recordings (Jali Musa Jawara or Sona Diabate, for example) present their traditions unvarnished, often sounding as if they were recorded live in one take; it is only on albums of bigger bands playing dance-pop that one finds more painstaking production techniques. But *Dance My Children Dance* ("Abaana Bakesa" in the Lugandan language) offers the intimacy of small-group African folk along with the tightly crafted arrangements and overall feeling of synthesis found in only the finest of big-budget African recordings.

It is a tour de force for Samite, who plays Western and traditional flutes, marimba, thumb-piano, and the seven-stringed Ugandan *litungu;* he plays every instrument on the album except the occasional conga drum. Samite's singing voice is warm and engaging and the tracks behind it are carefully assembled. In every way, *Dance My Children Dance* is a real gem, rooted yet accessible, flawlessly melodic and very easy to listen to. It does not really fit in any given category yet; unlike a lot of world-music crossovers, it is a dynamic and one-of-a-kind statement of a unique musical worldview.

For a more straightforward taste of the Kenyan pop called *benga,* try Daniel Owino Misiani and his Shirati Band's *Benga Blast* (Virgin/Earthworks 91314-2) and the compilation *The Nairobi Beat: Kenyan Pop Music* (Rounder CD 5030). *Benga* is smoother and more cosmopolitan (in the European sense) than some other African styles, with a more pronounced jazz tinge to the instrumental solos.

OFRA HAZA

Like its Anglo-American big brother, Israeli pop music falls, for the most part, outside the bounds of this survey. Its traditional and vernacular sources are usually homogenized past recognition or packaged into a relentless false nostalgia. It is essentially federal music, imposed on its listeners in the name of mass consumption.

But sometimes there can be Israeli releases that speak to the world. One is Ofra Haza's *Fifty Gates of Wisdom* (Shanachie CD 64002), a skillful account of the music of Yemeni Jews from the time before their wholesale immigration into Israel. Ofra Haza is a major Israeli pop star of Yemeni descent, and she was finally able to more or less command her record company to allow her to record the music of her ancestral home. The result was both a commercial and critical success, an object lesson in how to update a traditional style without losing its essence.

Jews were strictly regulated in Yemen, proscribed even in private from playing any musical instruments. But they evolved an ecstatic vocal music called *diwan,* accompanied for the most part by beating on metal trays, that was part of large festive gatherings in the special guest rooms also called *diwan.* It was a music for both singing and dancing, and this album recreates the spirit of those events with carefully ar-

Ofra Haza. *Courtesy Shanachie Records*

ranged tracks that fill the music out—with horns, synthesizers, and other percussion—without for a moment losing the
simpler textures of the music's origins. Every track is dominated by the solo voice and the clanging of what is called in the
notes "metal percussion."

Diwan is strongly reminiscent of the *qawwali* singing of
Pakistan, both in the devotional nature of its lyrics and the
emphasis on virtuosic singing with negligible accompaniment.

Ofra Haza does not have the kind of voice one finds in the great *qawwali* singers; she has spent too much time in front of sensitive microphones murmuring her pop hits to the adoring multitudes. But her studio technique is solid enough to give a good account of this exciting music. *Fifty Gates of Wisdom* is an eloquent and well-crafted testimonial to this once-vibrant form. It is also available from Globestyle Records under the title *Yemenite Songs* (Globestyle CDORB 006).

Another Israeli singer in the "oriental" style is Haim Moshe, whose *Le Grand Chanteur Oriental D'Israel* (Atoll ATO 96.836) is perhaps not the technical or folkloric achievement that *Fifty Gates of Wisdom* is, but is still a worthwhile document of the more esoteric side of Israeli music.

DISSIDENTEN

The first European band to draw extensively on the music of Northern Africa was Dissidenten, a Berlin group that has created an otherworldly mix of influences ranging as far afield as the Jakouka pipers of Morocco and psychedelic rock bands like Tangerine Dream or Pink Floyd. Dissidenten, the brainchild of producer/engineer/drummer/synthesizerist Marlon Klein, speaks less to North African Arabs than to Germany's *gastarbeiters* ("guest workers") of Arab descent and, especially, to their children.

Dissidenten's music takes the melodies and textures of various North African folk styles and adds more straightforward rock and funk beats—not unlike 3 Mustaphas 3 but without any of the humor—and then washes everything in tastefully programmed synthesizers. Their first album, *Life at the Pyramids* (Shanachie CD 64001), contains some compelling music—a little *rai*, a little funk, a little space-rock, even some Zimbabwean *mbira* from guest artist Stella Chiwese. But everything is held together by the band's vision of world culture and their roots in so many musics.

The more recent *Sahara Elektrik* (Shanachie CD 64005)

abandons the three-minute song format of *Life at the Pyramids* and ventures into more expansive sonic territory. Recorded in Tangier and Casablanca, it features fewer guest musicians playing ethnic instruments, opting instead for a core group playing drums, guitars, keyboards, and flute. But the world-music roots are very much there. The rock tinge is mostly just that—a tinge—and even when it is more than a tinge the music is intelligent, forthright, and often moving.

HAMZA EL DIN

Hamza El Din has been recording off and on since the sixties, developing a high enough profile in this country that he came to the attention of the Grateful Dead, who asked him to open the series of concerts they performed in front of the Great Pyramid of Cheops in Egypt in 1978. As a result of that meeting, Grateful Dead drummer Mickey Hart produced *Eclipse* (Rykodisc RCD 10103) for his acclaimed ethnic-music series "The World."

Din is a Nubian, born in the Sudan. Nubian music traditionally has been devoted to unaccompanied voice or to the *tar*, the round, flat polychromatic drum of the upper Nile region. But Din followed his muse into Egpyt to study the *oud*, precursor of the European lute (*"al'oud"* in Arabic), in Alexandria.

Eclipse is a quiet but intense excursion through the various musical territories Din now calls home. Some pieces are solo explorations of the *oud*'s unique timbres, others overdubbed collages of *oud, tar,* handclaps, and singing. Din sings softly but with precise articulation and a passionate yearning quality in his voice. His *oud* playing is equally deliberate and equally atmospheric. Another worthwhile Hamza El Din release is *A Song of the Nile* (JVC VID 25007).

As part of his "The World" series, Mickey Hart also produced *The Music of Upper and Lower Egypt* (Rykodisc RCD 10106), a more folkloric sampling of the various musical subcultures of the Nile basin. Like many such surveys, *The Music of Upper and Lower Egypt* lacks a sustained focus (the geographical area it covers is so large that individual performances have little in common with each other), but it serves the student of the region as an excellent research tool and the album *sounds* great. Hart is perhaps the finest on-location recording engineer working today. Another good collection from this region is *Musicians of the Nile: Luxor to Isna* (Virgin/RealWorld 91316-2).

DISCOGRAPHY

***Pop-Rai and Rachid Style* (Virgin/Earthworks 91407-2)
Chaba Fadela and Cheb Sahraoui: *Hana Hana* (Mango CCD 539856)
Cheb Mami: *Prince of Rai* (Shanachie CD 64013)
**Samite: *Dance My Children Dance* (Shanachie CD 65003)
Daniel Owino Misiani and his Shirati Band: *Benga Blast* (Virgin/Earthworks 91314-2)
The Nairobi Beat: Kenyan Pop Music (Rounder CD 5030)
**Ofra Haza: *Fifty Gates of Wisdom* (Shanachie CD 64002)
Haim Moshe: *Le Grand Chanteur Oriental D'Israel* (Atoll ATO 96.836)
Dissidenten: *Life at the Pyramids* (Shanachie CD 64001) and *Sahara Elektrik* (Shanachie CD 64005)
Hamza El Din: *Eclipse* (Rykodisc RCD 10103) and *A Song of the Nile* (JVC VID 25007)
The Music of Upper and Lower Egypt (Rykodisc RCD 10106)
Musicians of the Nile: Luxor to Isna (Virgin/RealWorld 91316-2)

**Highly recommended

Márta Sébestyén. *Courtesy Hannibal/Rykodisc*

4

~~~~~~~~~~~~~~~~~~~~~~~~~~~~~~~~~~~

EASTERN EUROPE

THE FOLK MUSIC OF many Eastern European countries, especially those lying south of the Danube, sounds seductively Oriental to Western ears. Rhythms are fractured into unusual-sounding time signatures: seven beats to the measure, or nine, or eleven (and still people dance to it!), where Western music is usually confined to four beats to the measure, or three. Singers produce their vocal tones in unusual ways, ignoring standard Western head and chest tones in favor of the almost exclusive use of the hard palate and nasal passages. Harmonies are constructed out of eerie-sounding minor modes with flat sixths, flat ninths, minor sevenths, then played and sung with such gusto that the effect can be nothing but cheerful.

And yet this is a European music in the end. The instruments are variants on the pipes, flutes, and viols of other European traditions. And Western art music has echoed to the strains of these harmonies from Liszt to Bartók to the present day. It is music with a secret, the closest I have come to finding a style that seems to have been dropped from outer space. It is no wonder that one of the most popular Eastern European albums is called *Le Mystère des Voix Bulgares* ("The Mystery of Bulgarian Voices").

The mystery is traceable, to the extent that one wants to trace it, to the music of Turkey, and the Ottoman Empire that flourished in the centuries before the European Renaissance. For 500 years the Ottomans ruled from Algeria in the west to Persia in the east and north as far as the gates of Vienna, centered in the greatest of all imperial cities: Istanbul. Possessed of the dominant military machine of the day, the Ottoman Turks were less interested in oppressing conquered territories than they were in conquering new territories. So they often hired administrators from the local populations, set up their own judicial system, organized the taxes, then rode off to find someone else to fight. As a result, localized cultures, especially in the Balkans, were, for the most part, left intact to absorb the Ottoman influence in their own way.

The result was a series of regional fusions—in Anatolia, Greece, Macedonia, Bulgaria, the Balkans, and elsewhere— that accommodated the prevailing cultural impulses from the capital while remaining true to local influences. And today the music benefits from that diversity in ways that the music of Western Europe, with its long history of cultural obliteration, cannot.

LE MYSTÈRE DES VOIX BULGARES

That said, we start not with Turkish music but with the release that sparked the current interest in Eastern European music, the spectacular three-volume series of Bulgarian choral music known as *Le Mystère des Voix Bulgares* (Elektra/Nonesuch 79165-2; *Volume 2* Elektra/Nonesuch 79201-2; *Volume 3* Fontana 846626-2). The chorus that made the albums is called the Bulgarian State Radio and Television Female Vocal Choir, a name of truly Stalinist clunkiness, so it is no surprise that promoters of the albums and subsequent tours would scramble to come up with an all-embracing title that had a little more style.

The twenty-three women of the choir sing in distinctively hard, narrow tones, given an added resonance in the recording studio that results in sheets of sound interacting with aural space in unusual ways. The reaction this produces in a concert audience is almost physical, as the nasal tones, without discernable vibrato (at least in the Western sense—although sometimes a singer will use a quavering attack that worries a single note over as much as two whole steps), join in dense chords, with five or six different intervals in a single octave. As the overtones merge and part and merge again, people's necks stretch and their shoulders hunch as they try to get around the music.

The albums feature songs from the various regions of Bulgaria: the whooping solo and duet pieces of the Shope region, mournful chorales from the mountains of Rhodope and Strandzha, brisk worksongs from the plains of Tourlak. Sometimes there is instrumental accompaniment, featuring *kaval* (a long wooden flute played lengthwise, like a recorder), *tambura* (a long-necked mandolin), *gadulka* (a small viol played upright from the chest), and the *gaida* bagpipes. Solo numbers have a more distinctly traditional feel, while many of the full-chorus pieces are obviously arranged. Occasionally, typical Bulgarian harmonic devices like the use of seconds and minor sevenths resolve into chords that echo instrumental modernists like Stan Kenton or Duke Ellington or the pioneering double-octet vocal arrangements of Herbert Spencer from the late 1940s.

But however much polish has been added in recent years, this is still a genuine folk music that carries with it a genuine sense of place and history. The unearthly grandeur and expressiveness of these voices could only be the product of a strong regional culture, lovingly cultivated.

Three of the principal soloists from the Bulgarian State Radio and Television Female Vocal Choir have released a trio album under the name Trio Bulgarka. *The Forest Is Crying* (Hannibal HNCD 1342) gives each vocalist room for individual workouts as well as plangent trio singing. The Shope region, with its solo and duet tradition, is particularly well-represented. Yanka Rupkina, the Strandzha belle who is arguably the best-known of the three, has a solo album called *Kalimenko Denko* (Hannibal HNCD 1334). And *Balkana: The Music of Bulgaria* (Hannibal HNCD 1335) is an excellent compilation that gives equal time to Bulgaria's vocal traditions and its distinctive instrumentals, including some spectacular *gaida* piping. As Richard Thompson once said, "Oooh, it gives me chills."

Another all-female choir, this one with seventy-six singers, is the Latvian Women's Choir, whose *Dzintars: Songs of Amber* (Rykodisc RCD 10130) was produced by Jerry Garcia and Mickey Hart of the Grateful Dead for Hart's ethnomusicological series "The World." Latvia being a Baltic state, *Dzintars* adheres to a more northern tradition, without the Ottoman influence that gives the singers of *Le Mystère* such exotic charm. But the production—as always in this series—is squeaky-clean, with a wonderfully atmospheric use of the ambient sounds of the recording location, filmmaker George Lucas's Skywalker Ranch. And the performances are heartfelt and affecting.

TURKISH MUSIC

Probably the best place to start for serious Turkish music is *Masters of Turkish Music* (Rounder CD 6041), an anthology of recordings made early in this century, in the twilight of the empire, by the greatest figures in Ottoman court music, the folk music of Anatolia, and the nightclub music of urban Istanbul. In them you can hear, sometimes with startling clarity, echoes of modern favorites from Muzsikás to 3 Mustaphas 3.

The vocal music of the court is called *gazel,* pieces sung with great passion and minimal accompaniment, resembling the classical music of northern India in that the artistry comes from the ability to improvise within a rigidly defined series of traditional modes and meters. It is sung by both women and men, and not just by native Turks, but by members of any of a number of minority groups, including Shephardic Jews. The strictures of the music are rigid enough that individual styles and approaches do not obscure the overriding unity of the form.

The rural folk music of the Anatolian peninsula is devoted mostly to instrumental workouts called *taksim,* often solo, on stringed instruments like the *ud* (spelled *oud* in some other countries), the *tanbur* (called *tambura* elsewhere), or the Turkish violin or cello. Some of these improvisations, especially those on the three-stringed *tanbur,* can be as breathtakingly fast and furious as a jazz-rock guitar solo by John McLaughlin or as languid and hypnotic as the guitar-*ragas* of John Fahey or Robbie Basho.

The urban nightclubs tend to feature larger groups, with wild soloists on clarinet (Sükrü Tunar) or violin (Nick Doneff, who has made a reputation in the United States). These are often "danceable" in the sense that hired dancers can negotiate the tricky rhythms without falling over.

Considering both the primitive sound quality (most of these sides were made before the advent of electronic recording) and the "exotic" nature of the music, at first most American listeners will find it hard to tell one song from another. But with repeated listening (and the help of the detailed liner notes) the music's particularities will emerge. *Masters of Turkish Music* is a haunting and unique collection.

A more recent recording, and thus a little easier on the ear, is *One Man's Passion* (Shanachie CD 65004) by the modern *ud* master George Mgrdichian. For this unusual package, Mgrdichian took a series of devotional songs written by an early Ottoman nobleman and concentrated on the melodies, playing them in a small ensemble of *uds,* percussion, and other stringed instruments and leaving a lot more room for improvisation than the usual *ud* ensemble. The result is a good showcase for Mgrdichian's astonishing virtuosity, sometimes sounding like a jam session among American jazz musicians but never losing its distinctive regional flavor.

Among other modern sessions, *The Art of the Ottoman Tanbur* (Gallo CD 586) by Abdi Coskun and Fahreddin Çimenli is a good collection of *taksims*. For traditional vocal songs accompanied by *saz*—the Turkish equivalent of the Greek *bouzouki*—try either Ozkan Talip's *Mysteries of Turkey* (Music of the World CDT 115) or Bayram Bilge Toker's *Turkish Folk Songs and Sufi Melodies* (Music of the World CDT 122).

Sufis, Islamic mystics from Eastern Anatolia and Persia, have played an important part in the development of Turkish music. Much of the high-court music of the Ottomans, especially their devotional music, was made by Sufis, and one of the most famous tourist attractions in Turkey, the whirling dervishes, are performing a Sufi rite. Principal instruments of Sufi music are the frame drum—a flat, one-headed hand drum similar to the North African *tar* and Celtic *bhodran*—and the *ney,* a long wooden flute played lengthwise, precursor to the Bulgarian *kaval.* In the hands of a master, the *ney* is an amazingly expressive instrument, capable of bending notes in ways a Western flutist would find impossible.

Kudsi Erguner. *Courtesy CMP Records*

Kudsi Erguner is such a master. His *Sufi Music of Turkey* (CMP CD 3005) gives a generalized view of the form while, under the name of the Erguner Brothers of Turkey, his album *The Mystic Flutes of the Sufis: Preludes of Ceremonies for Whirling Dervishes* (JVC Ethnic Sound Series VID 25005) gives a specific look at the kind of music played for the ecstatic dancers.

3 MUSTAPHAS 3

Over the last couple of years, the British-based sextet 3 Mustaphas 3 has built a significant audience in this country. Their music is a heady amalgam of Balkan and Anatolian styles (with a liberal sprinkling of African and Central Asian flavorings) sung in a babel of languages over a variety of strong drum patterns. Wholesale genre-bending and ornate musical puns are the rule, which means that if a song starts out as western swing you can be pretty sure the lyrics will be sung in Japanese.

The rhythm section of trap drums and electric bass guitar supports varying frontline configurations, most including accordion or piano, various wooden flutes or bagpipes, clarinet (sometimes saxophone), and the custom-made electric *bouzouki* of Hijaz Mustapha, whose striking solo work on the more extended instrumentals combines the lyricism and structure of Richard Thompson with the advanced harmonics of avant-noise guitarists like James "Blood" Ulmer. Like the Louisiana Cajun group Beausoleil, 3 Mustaphas 3 know how to broaden an ethnic style without losing sight of the strengths of the style itself. At times the rhythm section kicks like the Stax/Volt R&B backup band of the sixties, but the melodies never lose their Levantine flavor, and even when 3 Mustaphas 3 sound most like a rock band they always sound like a rock band with a firm understanding of their music's ethnic underpinnings.

Along with the music, the public has also come to enjoy the

3 Mustaphas 3. *Courtesy Rykodisc*

Myth of Mustapha as proclaimed over the years by the Mustaphas themselves, their management, and assorted publicists. The stories hold that the six Mustaphas—Niaveti Mustapha III (flutes, bagpipes, accordions); Daoudi Mustapha (clarinets and saxophones); Sabah Habas Mustapha (bass); Hijaz Mustapha (violin, electric *bouzouki,* guitars); Houzam Mustapha (drums and percussion); and Kemo "Kem Kem" Mustapha (keyboards and accordion)—are all half-brothers from a little Balkan hamlet called Szegerely, sometimes referred to as "the Balkan Brigadoon." There, legend has it, they began playing in a local nightclub called the Crazy Loquat Club. Taken in hand by their wise uncle, Patrel Mustapha, they were smuggled out of the country hiding in a shipment of refrigerators, hence their frequent onstage exhortation, "Take it to the fridge!" In this recounting of events, seekers after ultimate, objective truth may very well be disappointed.

Of their most recent sessions, the 1989 *Heart of Uncle* (Rykodisc RCD 20156) ranges the widest through the musics of the world and is also the most "produced," precisely layering instruments like the Ethiopian talking drum or a Western string quartet into tracks dominanted by *kaval* flute or *conjunto*-style accordions.

But when the group toured that year in support of the album, most observers, this one included, found them much more of a "live" band than *Heart of Uncle* would suggest. Their follow-up, *Soup of the Century* (Rykodisc RCD 10195), comes closer to matching the stripped-down energy of their shows. And while *Heart of Uncle* is a more consistent piece of work, *Soup of the Century* boasts higher high points, from the addled western swing of "Soba Song" (with lyrics in Japanese and English) to the accordion workout "This City Is Very Exciting!" (lyrics in Hindi). More accessible than other 3 Mustaphas 3 records, *Soup of the Century* is a perfect introduction to this group's exotic, passionate dance music, its melodies so haunting and unusual that one feels transported from Memphis, Tennessee to Memphis, Egypt.

MÁRTA SÉBESTYÉN AND MUZSIKÁS

Perhaps the most appealing pin-up in all of world music is the beautiful Hungarian singer Márta Sébestyén, a mere slip of a girl with an impish smile and a voice that combines the biting clarity of the great Bulgarian singers with qualities more often associated with Anglo-American folk divas: the sweetness of an Anna McGarrigle and the liquid phrasing of a Sandy Denny. You may have caught a glimpse of Sébestyén in the opening sequence of the 1987 film *The Music Box,* starring Jessica Lange.

Muzsikás, the group she sings with, draws on Hungarian traditional music in much the way sixties-era British folk groups like Pentangle drew on British traditional music, mixing and matching tunes and texts and making instrumen-

Muzsikás. *Courtesy Hannibal/Rykodisc*

tal interludes out of country dances. But, unlike Pentangle, Muzsikás uses no guitars at all. The instruments strumming in the background are mostly *bouzoukis,* with some reinforcement from duet violins, hurdy-gurdy, zither, and string bass. Instrumental solos are usually taken by various Balkan pipes and horns.

The resulting textures are remarkably rich and expressive. This is a deeply emotional music, filled with gorgeous and unusual melodies. *The Prisoner's Song* (Hannibal HNCD 1341) is the group's most consistent album, plangent ballads giving way to more driving numbers that sometimes stray into the off-center time signatures of Balkan music. *Blues for Transylvania* (Hannibal HNCD 1350) is another good one, and Márta Sébestyén has a solo album, entitled *Muzsikás* (Hannibal HNCD 1330), that is essentially indistinguishable from a Muzsikás album.

IVO PAPASOV

Perhaps the wildest take on the crazy-Balkan-time-signature syndrome comes from Ivo Papasov and His Bulgarian Wedding Orchestra. Papasov is a clarinet virtuoso whose American and European audiences are often studded with jazz luminaries, jaws dropping at the sheer impossibility of it all. Papasov's frantic modern-jazz solos on clarinet ride over time schemes like 9/8 and 7/4, with equally hot solos from alto saxophone and accordion and then some James Brown-style funky guitar. Both his CDs—*Orpheus Ascending* (Hannibal HNCD 1346) and *Balkanology* (Hannibal HNCD 1363)—will

Ivo Papasov. *Courtesy Hannibal/Rykodisc*

keep you dancing even while they make you feel that one of your legs is shorter than the other.

Not everyone will like these CDs. They may strike the terminally laidback as a bit . . . *strident*. But jazz fans should eat it up, if only for the chops, and I wouldn't be surprised if today's rebellious young persons went for it, too. It sounds like the perfect music to bug your parents with. Wait until they get used to Heavy Metal and then slip 'em some of *this!*

It could also have the opposite effect. Parents who want to be hipper than their kids could lay a little Ivo on 'em. It isn't hard to imagine tattooed young poodle-rockers shouting at their grooving folks, "Turn down that damned noise! Why can't you listen to something we can understand?"

ANNABOUBOULA

The music of Eastern Europe even invades the hip-hop house-music scene with the Greek-American band Annabouboula (you couldn't call them "bicoastal," exactly—maybe "multi-oceanic"). Producer Chris Lawrence, singer Anna Paidoussi, and guitarist George Sempepos spend less time playing actual Greek instruments than they do sampling old records and factoring in melodies from a Greek style known as *rembetika,* folk songs associated with the hashish-smoking bohemian underclass of large Aegean seaports.

Their two CDs *Greek Fire* (Shanachie CD 64027) and *In the Baths of Constantinople* (Shanachie CD 64022) are abstract in the fashion of house music. The instruments are rendered in splashes of texture through modern sampling technology, with a strong disco-style beat and intense, anguished singing from the operatically trained Paidoussi.

Annabouboula has achieved considerable success on the Greek pop scene, trampling underfoot the various progressive rock bands on the Greek charts, and their sights are quite evidently set on the American charts as well. Whether the house-music treatment can be applied to ethnic forms without turning them into grist for the media mill remains to be seen. Some would argue that this form of dance music has arisen from its various urban communities in a natural and organic enough way to make it an indigenous form and not an imposed demographic strategy. While waiting for the jury to come in, some of these cuts would be fun to play at parties.

KLEZMER

Although *klezmer* music, the slap-happy Yiddish jazz that began attracting attention among folk revivalists and record collectors in the middle seventies, is played mostly by American bands nowadays, it began in the ghettos of Poland and Russia early in this century as Jewish clarinetists and fiddlers began absorbing American jazz. The process is analagous to African or Caribbean musicians retooling rhythm and blues, except that where African groups playing *reggae* are joining a regional scene already in progress (see chapter 6, The Caribbean Islands), *klezmer* music now barely exists in the countries that gave it birth. All the *klezmer* groups named here are American.

The group that first opened most peoples' ears to the music was the Klezmorim, whose *Jazz Babies of the Ukraine* (Flying Fish FF 465) is a wild and wacky odyssey through the roots of the music in mock-travelogue form. The fact that the Klezmorim make everything they do so funny should not be interpreted as a lack of musical depth on their part. *Klezmer* music, with its circus rhythms, wild clarinet flights, and prevailing sense of reckless abandon, is undeniably comic, and the Klezmorim understand this perfectly. Their earliest recordings, collected on *First Recordings 1976–78* (Arhoolie CD 309), remain the most coherent statement yet of this still-growing form.

Perhaps the most advanced musicianship in *klezmer* is to be found in the Andy Statman Klezmer Orchestra and in the Klezmer Conservatory Band. These two groups take slightly different approaches based on their musical backgrounds. The Klezmer Conservatory Band, as their name implies, is made up of classically trained musicians for whom this music is a chance to let their hair down a little. Andy Statman's hair, on the other hand, has always been down. Statman, one of the great eclectics of the American folk scene, got his start playing the mandolin in bluegrass groups, falling in with young bluegrass players from the Northeast who were experimenting with jazz. Statman became the most commited modernist of them all, often called "the Ornette Coleman of the mandolin." Klezmer eventually became Statman's passion, but he remains a fine all-around player for whom taking musical chances has become a way of life, as *The Andy Statman Klezmer Orchestra* (Shanachie CD 21004) demonstrates.

The group Kapelye, led by *klezmer* scholar Henry Sapoznik, performs a mix of Yiddish theatrical songs from the turn of the century, along with *klezmer* instrumentals. Their more traditional approach to the music is available on *Chicken* (Shanachie CD 21007).

Two albums of Yiddish music from Eastern Europe that are not exactly *klezmer* are the Golden Gate Wedding Orchestra's program of traditional Jewish wedding music, *The Travelling Jewish Wedding* (Rykodisc RCD 10105), a happy-go-lucky collection of vocals and instrumentals; and the more serious *Partisans of Vilna: Songs of World War II Jewish Resistance* (Flying Fish FF 70450), compiled by Henry Sapoznik. *Partisans of Vilna* is no downer—it is not so much somber as fierce. And the singing (by men, women, and at times children) has some truly uplifting moments.

DISCOGRAPHY

The Bulgarian State Radio and Television Female Vocal Choir: *Le Mystère des Voix Bulgares Volume 1* (Elektra/Nonesuch 79165-2); *Le Mystère des Voix Bulgares Volume 2* (Elektra/Nonesuch 79201-2); and *Le Mystère des Voix Bulgares Volume 3* (Fontana 846626-2)

Trio Bulgarka: *The Forest Is Crying* (Hannibal HNCD 1342)

Yanka Rupkina: *Kalimenko Denko* (Hannibal HNCD 1334)

**Balkana: The Music of Bulgaria* (Hannibal HNCD 1335)

The Latvian Women's Choir: *Dzintars: Songs of Amber* (Rykodisc RCD 10130)

Masters of Turkish Music (Rounder CD 6041)

George Mgrdichian: *One Man's Passion* (Shanachie CD 65004)

Abdi Coskun and Fahreddin Çimenli: *The Art of the Ottoman Tanbur* (Gallo CD 586)

Ozkan Talip: *Mysteries of Turkey* (Music of the World CDT 115)

Bayram Bilge Toker: *Turkish Folk Songs and Sufi Melodies* (Music of the World CDT 122).

Kudsi Erguner: *Sufi Music of Turkey* (CMP CD 3005)

The Erguner Brothers of Turkey: *The Mystic Flutes of the Sufis: Preludes of Ceremonies for Whirling Dervishes* (JVC Ethnic Sound Series VID 25005)

3 Mustaphas 3: *Heart of Uncle* (Rykodisc RCD 20156) and **Soup of the Century* (Rykodisc RCD 10195)

Muzsikás: ***The Prisoner's Song* (Hannibal HNCD 1341) and *Blues for Transylvania* (Hannibal HNCD 1350)

Márta Sébestyén: *Muzsikás* (Hannibal HNCD 1330)

Ivo Papasov and His Bulgarian Wedding Orchestra: *Orpheus Ascending* (Hannibal HNCD 1346) and *Balkanology* (Hannibal HNCD 1363)

Annabouboula: *Greek Fire* (Shanachie CD 64027) and *In the Baths of Constantinople* (Shanachie CD 64022)

The Klezmorim: *Jazz Babies of the Ukraine* (Flying Fish FF 465) and **First Recordings 1976–78* (Arhoolie CD 309)

The Andy Statman Klezmer Orchestra (Shanachie CD 21004)

Kapelye: *Chicken* (Shanachie CD 21007)

The Golden Gate Wedding Orchestra: *The Travelling Jewish Wedding* (Rykodisc RCD 10105)

Partisans of Vilna: Songs of World War II Jewish Resistance (Flying Fish FF 70450)

**Highly recommended

Seamus Egan. *Courtesy Shanachie Records*

5
WESTERN EUROPE

CELTIC MUSIC

Both in terms of public consciousness and of the sheer cumulative weight of available product, the music of Western Europe is dominated by what has come to be called Celtic music (the "C" is hard), the instrumental and vocal music of the ancient druidic tribes of the British Isles. Although there are other traditionalist and fusion-oriented styles extant, the music of Ireland and Scotland—as well as Celtic-derived music from Wales, France, and England—now speaks to many white Americans as their ancestral harmony, even if their family line is mostly Norman or Saxon and even if their parents conceived them to the strains of Rossini.

Irish and Scottish music played a large part in the folk-music boom of the fifties and sixties, led first by the Clancy Brothers with Tommy Makem and later by the Chieftains, but when you say "Celtic music" what comes to the mind of today's fan are groups like Planxty, the Bothy Band, De Danaan, the Battlefield Band, and Clannad—the groups of the so-called "Celtic revolution."

In the seventies, inspired in part by hippie folk-rock bands like the Incredible String Band and Fairport Convention (about whom more later), a number of Celtic groups—most would say that the first was the legendary Planxty—began to break away from what had become a fairly rigid format. The first big change involved the instrumentation: around the traditional pipes, flutes, and fiddles there grew an increasingly forceful and varied guitar accompaniment. Following this, fretted instruments borrowed from other cultures (the Greek *bouzouki,* the Puerto Rican *quatro*) or from antiquity (the *cittern*) began to substitute for the guitar in an attempt to find new, often lighter textures.

The other important development was the increasing choice by younger singers to sing in Gaelic, considered their "lost" native language by Irish and Scottish nationalists. The blurred consonants and smoky vowel sounds of this ancient tongue, almost entirely forgotten a generation ago, combined with the chiming guitars (or their substitutes) and the familiar fiddle and flute tunes, made a powerfully emotional statement, especially to Irish-Americans hungry for a heightened ethnic self-awareness.

The problem with the Celtic revolution is that, like most revolutions, it has reached a place where its partisans begin to wonder what comes next. Many longtime players are following their aging demographics into the soft-edged precincts of new-age, but this has yet to produce anything particularly listenable. However, young Seamus Egan, winner of several Irish awards for traditional fluting, has produced an album that neatly avoids this malaise. His strategy on *A Week in January* (Shanachie CD 65005) is simplicity itself: Egan ignores settings and concentrates wholly on the melodies, usually played solo on flute, tin whistle, or *uillean pipes.* For the occasional rhythm instrument he plays the tenor banjo, but this charming and tuneful collection is based on the enduring truth of Celtic music—that great melodies have a power and grace that allow them to work magic when played solo in the old style.

Among the first of the Celtic-revolution bands, and long my favorite, was the Battlefield Band. The Battlefield Band in particular went even farther afield than its contemporaries to re-animate traditional material by including the synthesized keyboards of Alan Reid, often playing his multiple instruments as a kind of exploded concertina. *Celtic Hotel* (Temple CMD 2002), one of their best, contains many sublime moments, especially the bagpipe and whistle interplay between Dougie Pinnock and Duncan McGillivray, and Alistair Russell's singing is always tuneful and emotional.

But on some of their albums, especially in-concert recordings, the stalwart Battlefielders include several songs less because they can play them well than because they can play them at all (it's hard to believe that anyone would rather listen to their version of "Land of 1,000 Dances" than Wilson Pickett's). One band that was able to impose enough order on their sets to create a recognizable identity was Silly Wizard, a more straightforward post-Planxty outfit whose greatest-hits collection *The Best of Silly Wizard* (Shanachie CD 79048) is the best place to start for them.

Most of the Celtic revolution groups have greatest-hits packages of one kind or another: *Clannad in Concert* (Shanachie CD 79030) is a good one, as is *The Best of De Danaan* (Shanachie CD 79047), *The Planxty Collection* (Shanachie CD 79012), *The Best of the Bothy Band* (Green Linnet GLCD 3001), and *The Best of the Tannahill Weavers 1979–1989* (Green Linnet GLCD 1100). A number of the leading lights from these groups have gone on to make solo and duo records of some interest. Look for names like Andy Irvine, John Cunningham, Phil Cunningham, Andy Stewart, Triona Ni Dhomhnaill, Micheál O'Domhnaill, Matt Molloy, Dónal Lunny, and Robbie O'Connell.

One of the most intriguing approaches to this music in recent years has come not from the folk ranks, but from the original-instruments movement in Western art music. The point made here is that many tunes now considered "traditional," and played with such proletarian gusto by Celtic groups, were first written by Scottish court musicians for dancing or the instruction of their aristocratic employers. It was only with the demise of the Scottish court that these tunes slowly made their way into wide popular use, often being joined with more recent 18th- and 19th-century texts to become "folk" songs.

The Baltimore Consort's *On the Banks of Helicon: Early Music of Scotland* (Dorian DOR 90139) is an exceptionally fine audiophile recording of tunes and songs taken directly from these sources. The Consort's aggregation of lutes, flutes, and viols may not be as rhythmically dynamic as the fiddles, whistles, and guitars of the Celtic groups, but their emphasis on the tunes—like Seamus Egan's, as previously stated—gives this collection a subtle charm.

FAIRPORT CONVENTION

But all talk of the Celtic revolution aside (it was, after all, essentially backward-looking in its focus), the groups that did to the traditional music of Western Europe what Mahlathini did to the traditional music of Southern Africa were the English folk-rock bands of the late sixties. And the group that came closest to the omni-eclectic use of sources that is the signature of today's world music was Fairport Convention.

Fairport began as an undistinguished transatlantic pop band, a fairly straightforward clone of American groups like Jefferson Airplane. But with the release in 1969 of *Liege and Lief* (A&M 75021-4257-2) the group came up with a blueprint for the combination of traditional texts, rollicking instrumental tunes, and backbeat rhythms that has driven a generation of subsequent bands. Traditional ballads like "Tam Lin" and

"Matty Groves," sung with authority and grace by Sandy Denny, build up a tremendous emotional and musical force. Jigs and reels, mostly used as interludes, kick and shake with unbridled energy. And original songs, many written or cowritten by Richard Thompson, perfectly meld modern and medieval sensibilities.

Fairport Convention 1970. L to r: Dave Pegg, Richard Thompson, Dave Mattacks, Dave Swarbrick, Simon Nicol. *Courtesy Hannibal/Rykodisc*

But what sets *Liege and Lief* apart from other efforts to achieve this synthesis (even those of the Fairports themselves) is that it was a one-of-a-kind combination of strong musical personalities, never to be repeated. Sandy Denny, perhaps the finest singer of her generation, left the group soon after *Liege and Lief* to pursue a solo career and then died in 1978 after falling down a flight of stairs. Bassist Ashley Hutchings left the band at about the same time as she did, forming Steeleye Span with Tim Hart and Maddy Prior and then continuing through a series of distinguished traditional-folk fusions, often using the name "the Albion Band."

With both its vocal-pop and traditionalist wings gone, the group muddled through for a while, putting greater emphasis on Richard Thompson's brilliant guitar work. The best document from this period, and the other necessary Fairport Convention album, is the 1970 concert recording *House Full* (not to be confused with the studio LP *Full House,* also recorded in 1970; Hannibal HNCD 1319), a blistering set that features some great playing, especially from drummer Dave Mattacks, whose accompaniments of Dave Swarbrick's fiddle tunes are the only use of trap drums in jig time that I have heard that actually add meaning to the pieces.

Individual band members have gone on to distinguished solo careers. Sandy Denny formed a new group, Fotheringay, and they made one album, *Fotheringay* (Hannibal CGCD 4426), a lovely piece of work mixing traditional pieces like "Banks of the Nile" with originals like "The Sea." She then moved on to a series of more pop-oriented solo albums through the mid-seventies.

A later incarnation of Steeleye Span. L to r: Peter Knight, Maddy Prior, Nigel Pegrum, Rick Kemp, Bob Johnston. *Courtesy Shanachie Records*

Steeleye Span was formed by Ashley Hutchings after he left Fairport Convention in an attempt to continue the folk-rock explorations of *Liege and Lief*. The first lineup lasted only six months, but the second—with Hutchings, guitarist Martin Carthy, vocalist Maddy Prior, guitarist Tim Hart, and fiddler Peter Knight—stayed together for two years, recording two albums, *Please to See the King* (Shanachie CD 79075) and *Ten Man Mop* (Shanachie CD 79049). The first CD is an all-electric interpretation of traditional ballads and songs; the second has a more acoustic tinge. Both are important documents in the history of British folk-rock. After Hutchings and Carthy left in 1972, the group became more mainstream, gaining greater commercial success at the cost of musical innovation.

Hutchings left Steeleye Span when it became a Fairport clone and formed the Albion Band. Many of their excursions into English folk-rock are now out of print, but *The History of Ashley Hutchings* (Hannibal HNCD 4802) reprises much of that material, and the magnificent *Morris On* (Hannibal CGCD 4406) is still available, featuring Hutchings, Thompson, Mattacks, and friends in a piquant fusion of rock instrumentation and morris-dancing tunes. Morris dancing, the male line-dancing (modern teams or sides now include women) of England's west country, is a stately spectacle dating from pagan times, the dancers belled at the knee and waving scarves or tapping sticks in time. *Morris On* sparked a renewed interest in the form throughout the English-speaking world and many communities, especially in New England, now have their own morris teams.

Richard Thompson pitched in on various group and reunion projects, and in 1980, he released *Strict Tempo* (Hannibal CGCD 4409), an album of instrumentals ranging through various dance traditions of the British Isles and including some plangent originals and an eccentric version of Duke Ellington's "Rockin' in Rhythm." But Thompson's reputation largely rests with albums made with ex-wife Linda, a startlingly emotional singer. Their most rewarding releases are *I*

Richard Thompson. *Courtesy Hannibal/Rykodisc*

Want to See Those Bright Lights Tonight (Carthage CGCP 4407), *Pour Down Like Silver* (Carthage CGCD 4404), and *Shoot Out the Lights* (Hannibal HNCD 1303). Thompson's most artistically successful solo album is *Hand of Kindness* (Hannibal HNCD 1313). With a band including the standard guitar, bass, and drums augmented by John Kirkpatrick's accordion and two sax players, Thompson creates a contemporary wedding of British, Cajun, fifties rock, and soul in songs about lost love, despair, and death, Thompson's favorite subject matter.

Much of Dave Swarbrick's post-Fairport work is now out of print, but he teams with the legendary Martin Carthy on the fine traditionalist excursion *Life and Limb* (Green Linnet GLCD 3052). Martin Carthy is every bit as important a figure as any here discussed. Consistently cited by Bob Dylan and Paul Simon, among other American folkies, as the source for many of the traditional tunes that were turned into folk-pop hits in the sixties ("Scarborough Fair," for one), he is possessed of a ringing, galloping guitar style that has been extraordinarily influential. Like Swarbrick's, most of Carthy's best work, both solo and with the great singing group the Watersons, is out of print in this country, so *Life and Limb* is doubly valuable. Some of his earlier albums are available on CD from Topic Records as imports.

THE INCREDIBLE STRING BAND

This pioneering sixties duo had a one-of-a-kind vision of world-Celtic music, using guitar, pennywhistle, harpsichord, and Indian instruments like the *sitar* and the harmonium. They were also able to write songs that sounded less like written songs and more like the traditional music of this new country-of-the-mind. *The Hangman's Beautiful Daughter* (Hannibal CGCD 4421) is their only album still in print but it is also their best, worth hearing for its eccentric humour and hippie natural-life fantasies.

After the group broke up, cofounder Robin Williamson went on to a distinguished career in Celtic folk, first with a group called the Merry Band and later under his own name. Although much of this material remains in print, the only album yet to be released on CD is *Winter's Turning* (Flying Fish FF 70407), a collection of seasonal songs recorded in 1986. *Winter's Turning* continues the small-group intimacy on which Williamson built his reputation, featuring *cittern,* hammer dulcimer, pennywhistle, border pipes, and his trademark reedy vocals on songs by William Shakespeare and King Henry VIII, among others. One of the most interesting features of this buoyant, tuneful collection is Williamson's use of synthesizer, which fits these songs perfectly, not just as a quasi-accordion as in the Battlefield Band but as an instrument in its own right, with its own distinct personality yet perfectly rooted in the sonic necessities of the form.

PENTANGLE

Built around the unique guitar styles of Bert Jansch and John Renbourn, an Arabic-flavored use of open tunings and unusual inversions that later figured prominently in the work of rock players like Stephen Stills and Jimmy Page, Pentangle created a delightful fusion of jazz, traditional English folk, North African, Indian, blues, and baroque influences that has not been duplicated since. Unfortunately, their breakthrough work of the late sixties is all out of print now, and those albums now available are reunion sessions from the eighties that are musically less interesting.

There are, however, some worthwhile solo releases available from Jansch (I've heard it pronounced "Jansh," "Janks," "Yanks," and "Yanch," this last the one I prefer) and the group's other guitar virtuoso, John Renbourn. Jansch's *The Ornament Tree* (Run River D21S-71365) is an all-traditional package, but the guitar parts are as unusual as one has come to expect from him: full of movement and surprises, unstinting in their emotional commitment, and ruggedly personal.

Of the several Renbourn releases still in print, only a few have been issued on CD, among them the three albums he has made with American ragtime guitarist Stefan Grossman: *Live* (Shanachie CD 95001-D), *The Three Kingdoms* (Shanachie CD 95006), and *Snap a Little Owl* (Shanachie CD 97003). Renbourn's oft-repeated comment "I started out trying to play like Big Bill Broonzy and I'm still trying" is called to mind by these bluesy sets, with Renbourn's snapping single-string leads equally at home in fiddle tunes, country blues, baroque, and Indian-flavored material.

MARLICORNE

All of this musical activity in England did not go unnoticed in France. Considering that country's rich history of indigenous music it would be a surprise if no one had come along and organized them into a world style. And of all who tried, Gabriel

Yacoub found the greatest success with his group Marlicorne. A guitarist and songwriter, Yacoub had first made a reputation with the harpist Alan Stivell, whose Breton-Celtic harp albums (none currently available on CD) were the precursor to the new-age music of Andreas Vollenweider and others.

With Marlicorne, Yacoub was able to indulge his taste for vocal music (indeed, their unaccompanied harmony singing is one of the glories of the group) and medieval instruments like the crumhorn, an early double-reed whose nasal overtones give an almost Balkan cast to the music. But Marlicorne also had an eye to modern technology, using synthesizers and the famous gizmotron, and even inventing their own instruments, like the kigophone: an ironing board strung with guitar strings played by picks mounted on a motorized wheel. The cumulative effect of all this ancient and modern wizardry was music "light" and "heavy" at the same time, atmospheric and undeniably French.

The best Marlicorne album that remains in print is the retrospective *Legende: Deuxième Epoque* (Hannibal HNCD 1360). Its nearly seventy minutes covers every phase of the group's career in enough depth that listeners can concentrate on just one area and still get their money's worth. Another group using French sources is Lo Jai, whose *Acrobates et Musiciens* (Shanachie CD 21009)—the title taken from the Léger painting reproduced on the cover—is a somewhat glossier pop confection with a lot of Gallic charm.

FLAMENCO AND GYPSY POP

A recent development in Europe has been the popularity of a kind of *flamenco*-pop, led by the all-Gypsy guitar and percussion group the Gypsy Kings. Although the guitar playing on their first release, *Gypsy Kings* (Elektra 60845-2), is often impressive, one is hard put to lose the feeling that this is a kind of tourist music, born in expensive Cote d'Azure cafés in which an aristocratic audience wears berets and sandals and

talks expansively of *vagabondage des vacances*. These overtones of ethno-kitsch were in no way dissipated when the first
single off their second album, *Allegria* (Elektra/Musician
61019-2), turned out to be a peppy version of the Las Vegas
chestnut "Volare."

But the Gypsy Kings are not the only oysters in this particular stew, thank the Lord. Although there are not as many
good young *flamencistos* as there are departed giants of the
form, there are good releases coming out here and there. One
of the best of the Gypsy groups is Ketama, made up of the son
and nephews of *flamenco* great Pepe Habichuela along with
the leading songwriter of the "new *flamenco*," José Soto. Their
album *Ketama* (Hannibal HNCD 1336) is filled with wild,
uncompromising music, using Latin percussion, harmony
singing, and hot guitar playing straight from the roots of old
Spain.

Another Gypsy guitar group from the *flamenco* haunts of
Seville is Pata Negra, centered around the Amador brothers,
Rafael and Raimundo. Their album *Blues de la Frontera* (Hannibal HNCD 1309) combines Gypsy guitar with electric blues
in the style of B. B. King, an interesting synthesis that provides many exciting moments.

But the most exciting and unusual synthesis yet heard from
a *flamenco* group is *Songhai* (Hannibal HNCD 1323), the fruit
of a chance meeting in London between Ketama and Malian
kora master Toumani Diabate, with the later addition of former Pentangle double-bassist Danny Thompson. The similarity of the *kora* to European harps combined with the African inflections of *flamenco* produces a bicultural music that
meets on a genuine middle ground. Diabate and the Habichuela cousins urge each other on to greater heights and much
of the playing here is breathtaking.

For a more straightforward approach to *flamenco*, listeners
should hear Pepe Habichuela's *A Mandeli* (Hannibal HNCD
1315). This leader of Granada's Carmona family of great guitarists has not been unaffected by his nephews' experiments in

Ketama: electric bass and Latin percussion make unostentatious appearances here. But he remains, along with Paco de Lucia, the leading *flamenco* guitarist in Spain and his playing here is often dazzling.

Early Cante Flamenco. *Courtesy Arhoolie Records*

But for genuine *flamenco* one must go back a generation or two. The best reissue of early *flamenco* recordings, in this case from the 1930s, is *Early Cante Flamenco* (Arhoolie CD 326). This hour-plus package contains vintage recordings by most of the greatest singers from the last generation of pure *flamenco* artists, including Niña de los Peines, instantly recognizable for her keening timbre and soulful interpretations, and Manuel Vallejo, whose emotional commitment, elastic phrasing, and sheer lung-power strain credulity.

DISCOGRAPHY

Seamus Egan: *A Week in January* (Shanachie CD 65005)
The Battlefield Band: *Celtic Hotel* (Temple CMD 2002)
The Best of Silly Wizard (Shanachie CD 79048)
Clannad in Concert (Shanachie CD 79030)
The Best of De Danaan (Shanachie CD 79047)
The Planxty Collection (Shanachie CD 79012)
The Best of the Bothy Band (Green Linnet GLCD 3001)
The Best of the Tannahill Weavers 1979–1989 (Green Linnet GLCD 1100)
The Baltimore Consort: *On the Banks of Helicon: Early Music of Scotland* (Dorian DOR 90139)
Fairport Convention: **Liege and Lief* (A&M 75021-4257-2) and *House Full* (Hannibal HNCD 1319)
Fotheringay (Hannibal CGCD 4426)
Steeleye Span: *Please to See the King* (Shananchie CD 79075) and *Ten Man Mop* (Shanachie CD 79049)
The History of Ashley Hutchings (Hannibal HNCD 4802)
**Morris On* (Hannibal CGCD 4406)
Richard Thompson: *Strict Tempo* (Hannibal CGCD 4409); *I Want to See Those Bright Lights Tonight* (Carthage CGCD 4407); *Pour Down Like Silver* (Carthage CGCD 4404); *Shoot Out the Lights* (Hannibal HNCD 1303); and *Hand of Kindness* (Hannibal HNCD 1313)
Dave Swarbrick and Martin Carthy: *Life and Limb* (Green Linnet GLCD 3052)
**Incredible String Band: *The Hangman's Beautiful Daughter* (Hannibal CGCD 4421)
Robin Williamson: *Winter's Turning* (Flying Fish FF 70407)
Bert Jansch: *The Ornament Tree* (Run River D21S-71365)
John Renbourn and Stefan Grossman: *Live* (Shanachie CD 95001-D); *The Three Kingdoms* (Shanachie CD 95006); and *Snap a Little Owl* (Shanachie CD 97003)
**Marlicorne: *Legende: Deuxième Epoque* (Hannibal HNCD 1360)
Lo Jai: *Acrobates et Musiciens* (Shanachie CD 21009)
The Gypsy Kings: *Gypsy Kings* (Elektra 60845-2) and *Allegria* (Elektra/Musician 61019-2)
Ketama (Hannibal HNCD 1336)

Pata Negra: **Blues de la Frontera** (Hannibal HNCD 1309)
**Songhai (Hannibal HNCD 1323)
Pepe Habichuela: **A Mandeli** (Hannibal HNCD 1315)
Early Cante Flamenco (Arhoolie CD 326)

**Highly recommended

Bunny Wailer. *Courtesy Shanachie Records*

6
THE CARIBBEAN ISLANDS

REGGAE

The music of the Caribbean Islands, like that of Western Europe, is dominated in the public mind and the record- store bins by one musical style: in this case the exhortative syncopations of *reggae,* once the obscure product of Jamaica's ghetto dancehalls and now a planetary voice for black nationalism and Solomonic spirituality. Both *calypso,* the improvising-songster tradition of Trinidad and other islands, and *salsa,* the big-band Latin dance music originating in Cuba (once called "Afro-Cuban" music), continue to produce vital and exciting new styles and performers, but the unique upside-down rhythms and herb-scented reveries of *reggae* found such a huge worldwide audience in the seventies that it is now thought of by outsiders as the primary music of the region.

From the earliest folk style—called *mento*—Jamaican music's signature has been an instantly recognizable "backwards" guitar strum. One has to assume that island musicians simply hear music that way, because it has become a perennial feature of the music. As Florida radio stations began beaming American rhythm and blues across the Straits of Florida, Jamaican "rude boys" started to play a hyped-up, blaring variation they called *ska. Ska* mutated into a style called "rock steady," and then into *reggae,* reflecting the overall trend in the popular music of the sixties away from facile entertainment and toward a more serious examination of art and life.

BOB MARLEY AND THE WAILERS

Although it cannot be said that he created it single-handedly, the towering figure in *reggae* remains the late Bob Marley, the music's greatest international star. The use of overt political and spiritual themes, often delivered from the perspective of Jamaica's Rastafarian ganga sect, did not originate with Marley. But Marley's abilities as a songwriter so far outstripped all other *reggae* artists, before or since, that he became the de facto voice of the movement; his passionate, articulate condemnations of the "Babylon system" and his pleas for unity, harmony, and peace striking nerves worldwide. He deserves a place beside Woody Guthrie, Bob Dylan, and very few others in the pantheon of the protest song.

Marley started from the bottom, living in squalid Kingston tenement yards and entering local talent contests with his group the Wailers, made up of Marley, his wife, Rita, and friends Peter Tosh and Neville "Bunny Wailer" Livingstone. He slowly built a recording career through the sixties, but it was while stranded in London in 1972 after the failure of a travelling revue of Jamaican groups that Marley attracted the attention of Chris Blackwell, an English producer of rock records who made Marley a star with the first Wailers album, *Catch a Fire* (Tuff Gong/Island 422-846201-2).

Marley's first four or five albums (with the departure of Tosh and Livingstone, the group changed its name to Bob

Marley and the Wailers) put *reggae*, Rastafari, and Jamaica on the musical map. The stoned-out Rasta worldview— benevolent and angry at the same time—struck a chord with disaffected young people around the world, and songs like "I Shot the Sheriff," "Get Up, Stand Up," "Lively Up Yourself," "Jammin'," and "Natty Dread" communicated that worldview brilliantly.

At the bottom of Marley's songs, the rhythmic grooves are solid, flexible, and infinitely varied, divergent pulses for each instrument coming together in a kind of fugue that produces some of the most supple musical movement ever recorded. And set to memorable melodies are lyrics whose colorful, quasi-Biblical argot lend an air of mystery that more straightforward political songwriters lack. Terms like "dread" are not admitting of easy definition. Is it "fear of God" (called "Jah" by the Rastas)? Is it the fear inspired in Babylon by those who serve Jah? Or is it the meditative trance induced by the Rastas' near-constant marijuana smoking (called "skanking"—often using the huge cigars known as "spliffs")?

But none of the trappings of *reggae*—the shoulder-length braids called dreadlocks, the veneration of Ethiopian emperor Haile Selassie and Jamaican-born black nationalist Marcus Garvey, or even the herb-holiness—would have made it anything more than a fad if Marley had not kept putting out great records. After *Catch a Fire,* in quick succession came *Burnin'* (Tuff Gong/Island 422-846200), then *Natty Dread* (Tuff Gong/Island 422-846204-2), and the fine in-concert album *Live* (Tuff Gong/Island 422-846203-2).

Marley and the band worked hard through the early and middle seventies, often recording two LPs per year and pursuing a grinding worldwide tour schedule. After a while, there came the inevitable decline in quality, with some later albums sounding tired and lacking inspiration. But Marley rallied in the late seventies and produced what may be his finest album, *Survival* (Tuff Gong/Island 422-846202-2). Ironically, it was soon after this that Marley was diagnosed with terminal cancer. After he died in 1981 a number of greatest-hits packages came out, the best of which is *Legend: The Best of Bob Marley and the Wailers* (Tuff Gong/Island 422-846210-2).

Since Marley's death, *reggae* (and the Jamaican music scene generally) has gone into a prolonged stall. Many Rastas complain that the Reagan-Bush drug eradication policy has devastated the Jamaican ganga crop while flooding the country with Colombian cocaine, a drug true Rastas consider unholy. But whatever the reason, a lot of records are released every year, few of any particular distinction. Elements developed by Marley have been ground into dust through overuse, and many of the new styles seem cheap and imitative. The chanted monologues known as "toasting" usually sound like watered-down American rap; the bigger bands, with their horns and electronic keyboards, often sound cheesy and commercial; and no one has come close to Marley's genius at writing black-nationalist lyrics that rise above the level of mere tracts to work as songs.

PETER TOSH AND BUNNY WAILER

After leaving the Wailers, Peter Tosh wrote some of the most hard-edged *reggae* songs of the seventies and eighties. Cold-blooded gangster odes like "Stepping Razor" stood in sharp contrast to the spiritual and political concerns of other singers of Marley's generation. His two best albums, *Legalize It* (Columbia CK 34253) and *Equal Rights* (Columbia EK 34670), are filled with tense, bilious meditations on violence and treachery, and these seem to be the overriding themes in his life as well. When Jamaican Prime Minister Michael Manley attended a large outdoor *reggae* concert in Kingston, Tosh virulently scolded him from the stage for his failure to legalize marijuana. A while later, Tosh was ambushed and severely beaten by an unidentified group of vigilantes. In 1987, he met a violent death when fringe members of his entourage broke into his house and murdered him along with two other people.

Bunny Wailer, the last surviving member of the original three Wailers, is a legendary figure in his own right (it is said he was the first of the group to wear dreadlocks). Born Neville O'Reilly Livingstone, he and Marley were boyhood friends but, after the Wailers' world tour of 1973, he resolved never to leave Jamaica again. Moving into the mountains and living in hermitlike seclusion, he finally emerged in 1987 to play a sold-out concert in Madison Square Garden.

Although many of the records he made in the seventies and early eighties were criticized for being too commercial, *Time Will Tell—A Tribute to Bob Marley* (Shanachie CD 43072) is profoundly serious, showcasing Bunny's prodigious skills as producer, arranger, and multi-instrumentalist. The songs range widely from early efforts like "I Shot the Sheriff" to one of Marley's last works, "Redemption Song." Long years of singing duets with Marley has given Bunny a hermetic understanding of Marley's phrasing and embellishments, and the result is an eerie re-creation of Marley's voice and manner.

Not exactly a greatest-hits collection, *Time Will Tell* has plenty of familiar numbers on it, chosen more for their place in the Marley canon than their position on the pop charts. "No Woman No Cry" and "Rebel Music" are included, but so is "War," Marley's transcription of Emperor Haile Selassie's 1943 speech to the United Nations General Assembly.

AUGUSTUS PABLO

One interesting trend that started in the seventies and has picked up steam through today's advanced studio technology is the trippy instrumental remixing known as "dub." Created for Jamaica's urban dancehalls and rural sound-system dances, dub records take the rhythm tracks from some of the most popular *reggae* records, strip them of their lead vocals, and overlay high-frequency textures of shimmering studio effects, shooting channels in and out in a bewildering display of engineering sleight of hand. As the drums and bass lope along unconcerned, a single guitar track will suddenly appear, go through various sonic contortions, and then disappear, replaced by the wordless chanting of a female chorus or by sound effects like hissing snakes, explosions, or gunfire.

Augustus Pablo. *Photo by David Corio, courtesy Shanachie Records*

One of the finest and most influential of the dub producers is Augustus Pablo, who likes to top off his tracks with solos on the melodica. Instrumental albums like *Blowing with the Wind* (Shanachie CD 43076) and *East of the River Nile* (Message CD 1003) could almost be considered new age instrumental music, while dub records like *Rockers Meets King Tubbys in a Fire House* (Shanachie CD 43001) are as lean and muscular as anyone's. In Pablo's hands, dub becomes a kind of funk minimalism that develops a tremendous hypnotic force through repetition and a tasteful use of effects.

Although *Rockers Meets King Tubbys in a Fire House* is one of the most enchantingly listenable *reggae* albums available, a good compilation for those who want to sample several different producers' styles is *Towering Dub Inferno* (Rykodisc RCD 20152), more than an hour of music from the vaults of Jamaica's ROIR Records.

JIMMY CLIFF

While the new generation of *reggae* musicians has not lived up to Marley's legacy (indeed, modern *reggae* is so pop-oriented now that it can hardly be called a world-music style at all), there are still fine albums available by artists who have survived the master. The first international star of *reggae* was Jimmy Cliff, whose soundtrack album to the *reggae*-scored Jamaican gangster film *The Harder They Come* (Mango CCD 9202) was many Americans' first taste of the music.

Cliff starred in the film and sang several songs in it, including the title tune, "You Can Get It If You Really Want," and "Sitting in Limbo," later covered by New Orleans funksters the Neville Brothers. The soundtrack album also contains some of the most popular *reggae* singles from the late sixties by groups like the Melodians and Toots and the Maytals.

TOOTS AND THE MAYTALS

Toots and the Maytals have had perhaps the longest career in *reggae,* spanning the early-sixties *ska* and rock-steady styles, their urgent three-part harmonies in those days often applied to hymns and other devotional material. They are still going strong today. "Toots" Hibbert's sweet, sunny personality will remind many of South Africa's Joseph Shabalala, leader of Ladysmith Black Mambazo, and his gritty, inspired singing is the equal to Otis Redding or any other American soul singer of the 1960s.

Funky Kingston (Mango CCD 9330) is a good place to start. It was the group's first album in this country, released to capitalize on the interest in *The Harder They Come,* and it contains a lot of great dance music, including inspired covers of American pop tunes like John Denver's "Country Roads" (substituting "West Jamaica" for "West Virginia") and the rock chestnut "Louie, Louie," itself a takeoff on Jamaican patois. *Reggae Got Soul* (Mango CCD 9374) was released a few years later as part of a major United States tour. It, too, is terrific party music, with more sophisticated production values (the engineering on *Funky Kingston* can be primitive in spots) and a greater emphasis on songwriting.

Toots Hibbert. *Courtesy Mango Records*

Unfortunately, that tour was not well-planned, including a series of arena dates opening for the Who in which the Maytals were sometimes booed off the stage by uncomprehending yokels, and their career never quite revived in this country. But some years later, Toots recorded a solo album, *Toots in Memphis* (Mango CCD 9818), that follows the brilliant but obvious course of combining his soulful singing with the famous Stax/Volt studio band on some of the great hits of American rhythm and blues. The results are predictably electrifying, both in terms of Toots's ability to remake well-known songs in his own image and the surprising ability of the Memphis musicians to pump out killer *reggae* tracks.

RAS MICHAEL

Although Marley was a Rastafarian, the musical traditions of the Rasta subculture (dating back well before Marley's birth) were rarely prominent in his music, so personalized was his

Ras Michael. *Courtesy Shanachie Records*

vision. Thus, one way out from under Marley's long shadow has been this more vernacular style. And perhaps its most adroit use can be found in albums by the master percussionist Ras Michael.

A leading exponent of the traditional Rasta hand-drumming known as *burra,* Ras Michael is also a highly charged and emotional singer. His 1989 CD, *Know Now* (Shanachie CD 64019), integrates the hypnotic polyrhythms of *burra* drumming into the more-or-less standard mix of trap drums, electric keyboards, and guitars so that there always seems to be something interesting percolating just under the threshold of hearing—the rhythms that most *reggae* tracks imply but do not actually state.

The songs on *Know Now* are less overtly engaged politically than they are spiritually, "Born in the Ghetto" saying "By living in it right/In Jah sight/I am not ashamed." And numbers like "Rastaman Give Thanks and Praise" and "Marriage in Canaan" pour out positive vibrations in a message of healing and grace that truly transcends genre, unusual in the largely self-referential world of *reggae*. Other Ras Michael albums worth hearing are *Rally Round* (Shanachie CD 43027), a collection of earlier recordings, and *Zion Train* (SST SSTCD 168).

BURNING SPEAR

Of all the political writers to flourish in Marley's shadow, one whose authority continues undiminished since Marley's death is Winston Rodney, better known by the stage name Burning Spear. Rodney has an uncanny ability to write simple melodies around repeating phrases that stick in the mind forever. He is also a spellbinding monologuist, as the performance of his song "Jah No Dead" in the great film *Rockers* shows. "They're trying to fool the black population/It's a rum-ah, a rum-ah, a rum-ah, yeh," he chants to the accompaniment of nothing but waves crashing on a deserted beach, "Jah no dead."

Any of his albums will contain stirring moments like these.

Burning Spear. *Courtesy Mango Records*

A 1990 release with better-than-average production values is *Mek We Dweet* (Mango CCD 539863), but anything with his name on it is worth getting. A good greatest-hits package is *Live In Paris* (Slash/Warner Brothers 25842-2). The soundtrack from the film *Rockers* (Mango CCD 9587), featuring various artists, is also available.

ALPHA BLONDY AND LUCKY DUBE

At the time of his death, Bob Marley was a respected musical force in Europe and North America, but his acceptance in those markets did not approach the veneration in which he was held in the Third World, especially in Africa. Given the strong vein of Pan-Africanism in his songs ("Africa Unite," "Exodus") it is no surprise that in the years since Marley's death a new generation of African *reggae* artists has emerged.

Alpha Blondy. *Courtesy Shanachie Records*

While modern Jamaican *reggae* flirts ever more dangerously with rap and pop, these African writers carry on the Marley tradition of polemical songwriting: angry lyrics with a mystical slant set to dynamic melodies accompanied by the familiar ponderous backbeat.

The Ivory Coast native Alpha Blondy was the first great African star of *reggae,* drawing six-figure crowds all over the continent through most of the eighties. His prominence is such that a peace concert he played on the border of Mali and Burkina Faso in 1986 helped keep the conflict between those two countries from escalating into war. Compared to the Jamaican variety, Blondy's Africanized *reggae* is more tuneful but not as rhythmically supple. He sings in English, French, Dioula, Hebrew, Arabic, and Mandique, his lyrics stressing global unity (he often sings alternate verses of the same song in Hebrew and Arabic) and resistance to oppression. There are good examples of his work on *Jerusalem* (Shanachie CD 43054) and *The Best of Alpha Blondy* (Shanachie CD 43075).

Although Blondy's music has been banned in South Africa for the last several years, it was heard often enough underground to inspire the next great African *reggae* star. Lucky

Dube (pronounced "DOO-Bay") was a successful star of Zulu pop music before changing to *reggae* in the hopes of reaching beyond Southern Africa with a message of unity.

On *Prisoner* (Shanachie CD 43073), he uses keyboards more extensively than previous *reggae* artists, building tracks that coo and burble behind his keening vocals. Dube is not afraid to apply rigorous standards of conduct both to politicians and to himself and his audience. The title song to *Slave* (Shanachie CD 43060) examines the evils of alcoholism. Other tracks examine the problems caused by absentee fathers. But Dube's principal theme is cultural unity through Rastafari and the constant struggle against false prophets and government repression. These meditations are sung in a gorgeous falsetto

Lucky Dube. *Courtesy Shanachie Records*

against meticulously prepared backing tracks as stately and rooted as Marley's own.

SKA

The term "ska" came from the scratching electric-guitar strum that defined the music in its beginnings in the early sixties. It was tough, cheap, noisy, violent music that spun off the occasional pop hit (like Millie Small's "My Boy Lollipop" or "The Israelites" by Desmond Dekker), but mostly it was the province of the Jamaican underclass, both in Kingston and in expatriate London. Many of the records were instrumentals based on blaring unison themes for trumpets and saxophones, often plagiarized from current pop hits, with the rhythms sent every which way.

Since almost all releases at the time were as 45s, the only re-issues available today are in compilations. The best of these is *More Intensified! Original Ska, Volume 2: 1963–1967* (Mango CCD 9597). More recent, and thus considerably less primitive than *Volume 1,* its sloppy dance grooves will show you a good time, especially if you're really drunk.

THE JOLLY BOYS

The recent rediscovery of the charming, loopy, *mento* folk group the Jolly Boys has added a lot to our understanding of the history of Caribbean music. Both of their albums, *Pop 'N' Mento* (Rykodisc RCD 10185) and *Sunshine 'N' Water* (Rykodisc RCD 10187), are filled with double-entendre songs about drinking rum, idling around the dockside, and the charms of complaisant island women. The fact that the cumulative ages of the group's four members total more than 250 years adds a certain wry charm to the proceedings.

It is tourist music by and large, loose-limbed and easy, but with no pretensions to anything more grand. The tenor banjo plunks out the melody, the guitar scratches along, and the old voices ask the musical question, "Who's going to do the bang-bang now that Lulu's gone away?"

GAZOLINE

Pier Rosier, founder of Gazoline, was born in French-speaking Martinique, where the traditional carnival music is called *chouval bwa* or "rocking horse." He formed Gazoline to inject this traditional rocking-horse rhythm into the island dance-pop known as *zouk*. Like so many attempts to vernacularize a popular music, the group was a huge success. *Zouk Obsession* (Shanachie CD 64021) is a collection of their biggest hits in Martinique. As such, it avoids the pitfalls of so many world-dance releases, which feature one or two smoking tracks surrounded with uninspired filler material. Every song on *Zouk Obsession* is hot and danceable, a big horn-heavy band punching out one lightning riff after another.

The similarity between the musics of former French colonies in Africa and the Caribbean has been noted in chapter 2. The similarity is apparent here as well, but Gazoline does not favor the light, guitar-driven attack of Haiti's Tabou Combo or Paris-based African groups like Loketo. Rosier prefers massed horns and synthesizers on top of a heavy, thumping beat and the result is a dance music that even Americans not used to world-beat rhythms can enjoy.

HAITIAN MUSIC

It is distressing that so little of the popular music of Haiti is available in this country, because Haitian dance-pop is the most irrepressible fusion currently being made on the planet. Although there is a healthy recording and performing scene both in Haiti and in the expatriate Haitian communities of New York City and elsewhere, and a number of terrific albums are available as imports, the only worthwhile CD release listed in *Schwann* is *Konbit—Burning Rhythms of Haiti* (A&M 75021-5281-2).

This excellent sampler, compiled by film director Jonathan Demme, documents a music whose high spirits and virtuosity belie generations of brutal dictatorship and poverty. The best songs on this album are played in the *compas-direct* style, combining the light, springy chromaticism of African pop music with the driving beat of North American rhythm and blues, especially the polyrhythmic funk of New Orleans groups like the Neville Brothers. The Nevilles appear on two cuts on the album, singing the title song and "San Nou Ki La" with Les Frères Parents, and it was their enthusiasm that convinced A&M Records to back the project. Other artists appearing on *Konbit* include the Magnum Band, Ensemble Nemours Jean-Baptiste (in two thirty-year-old performances that still sound fresh), and the legendary Tabou Combo.

Some of the retail record stores listed in Appendix B will certainly carry Haitian imports, or know where one can find them. And groups like Tabou Combo can be often found playing at large dances in any city with a good-sized Haitian community. I have been told that the atmosphere at these events is gracious and welcoming, the participants stylishly dressed and ready to enjoy a civilized night out, and the music and dancing spectacular.

But *Konbit* is the best place to start. It is an important collection for many reasons: for the opportunity it gives to Haitian musicians to address the political and social aspirations of their country to an international audience, for the opportunity it gives to the world to discover this little-known but incredibly dynamic music, and for another, more directly helpful reason—the producers and artists have arranged for a share of their royalties to create a fund to finance the creation of sanitary water supplies for rural communities in Haiti that do not have clean, available water.

Another release, so recent that it is not yet listed in *Schwann* as of this writing, is *Voudou Adjae* (Mango CCD 162-539-899) by the *rara* group Boukman Eksperyans. The *rara* style is more heavily African, with a greater emphasis on

Boukman Eksperyans. *Photo by Steve Winter, courtesy Mango Records*

drumming. It echoes the voodoo drum music that first came to light in Haiti nearly 200 years ago, with an overlay of guitars and keyboards playing in a more-or-less generic style. The focus here is on the drumming, and this young group has toured North America to considerable acclaim.

SALSA

With *salsa* music one is confronted with the opposite problem from that of Haitian music: there are just too many releases available to be adequately surveyed. For all its fire and brilliance, it is still basically a "pop" form, the established popular music of most of this hemisphere. Any city with a large Hispanic population will have several nightclubs, ballrooms, and radio stations whose sole purpose is the presentation of *salsa* music. It is featured prominently on the Spanish-language television networks offered by most cable companies. In this expansion from its roots in Cuban jazz, *salsa* has come to boast truly international superstars like the Fania All-Stars, Celia Cruz, Ruben Blades, Willie Colón, Tito Puente, and quite a few others. To North American ears, it remains an exotic style with deep roots, but still a question arises: How does a music that is this widely celebrated fit into a book whose main concern is telling its readers about music they haven't heard before?

Certainly, an entire book could be written about *salsa* alone; the Public Broadcasting System presented in 1991 a three-part history of the music called "Routes of Rhythm," hosted by Harry Belafonte. This excellent series has a two-CD companion set, *A Carnival of Cuban Music* (*Volume 1,* Rounder CD 5049; *Volume 2,* Rounder CD 5050), which contains many fine performances but suffers by trying to cover too much territory, from early Cuban roots-music to Xavier Cugat's glossy orchestra (vocals by Bing Crosby) to an in-concert recording of Ruben Blades' *salsa*-rock band.

For most people, *salsa* means a certain kind of beat—a beat subdivided into miniscule subsections by congas, timbales, shakers, and trap drums, often so precisely that the untrained ear has a hard time finding the downbeat. (It is hands down the most polyrhythmic music ever made.) Over these finely calibrated yet burning grooves is overlaid a big, brass-heavy horn section along with piano, electric bass, and the occasional guitar or *quatro*. Lyrics are always sung in Spanish, often with an exagerrated lower-class accent (Celia Cruz is great at that).

There are retail record stores listed in Appendix B where the neophyte can get some guidance about which are the best *salsa* albums to start with. My all-time favorites are the Fania All-Stars, in part because different singers are featured on different numbers, which keeps the whole thing from sounding too similar. Another personal icon is Ruben Blades, who brought a new sophistication to *salsa* songwriting and replaced the standard horn section with banks of synthesizers for a more modern sound. His *Buscando America* (Elektra 60352-2) is tuneful and thought-provoking, with some excellent support from his backup band, Seis Del Solar ("Six from the Tenement"). Blades also has an English-language album called *Nothing but the Truth* (Elektra 60754-2).

But the fact is, I do not think *salsa* can be adequately

surveyed here, short of devoting the entire book to the subject. In addition to the names listed above, other great *salsa* artists include Ray Barretto, Eddie Palmieri, Machito and his Afro-Cubans, and Daniel Ponce. Nothing could give me greater pleasure than to think a reader had found some great music through my efforts, but in the case of *salsa* I must forego that pleasure and another equally diverting one—the pleasure of pontificating on this subject further.

CALYPSO AND SOCA

The Caribbean music with the second-longest vogue among North American fans is *calypso,* the on-the-spot songwriting of the English-speaking islands, most notably Trinidad. Trinidadian stars like the Mighty Sparrow have taken *calypso* around the world, at first accompanied only by guitar, but later in large bands with slick arrangements. The songs are usually very funny, the instrumentalists smooth and genial.

But the original form has been eclipsed over the last ten years or so by *soca* (short for "soul *calypso*"), a synthesized dance-floor hybrid that keeps the signature meter of the original lyric style and adds repetitive choruses and electronic percussion effects. As a result, most of the best old *calypso* albums are out of print. Three compilations serve to document the history of the music: *Calypso Pioneers: 1912–1937* (Rounder CD 1039), *Calypso Breakaway: 1927–1941* (Rounder CD 1054-2), and *Calypsos from Trinidad* (Folklyric ARFL CD 7004). All feature colorfully named performers from *calypso*'s early years like Attila the Hun, Lord Beginner, the Executor, and Lovey's Orchestra.

An interesting evocation of that era is Van Dyke Parks' *Discover America* (Warner Brothers 26145-2), a mostly successful attempt by the Hollywood film-scorer and one-time Brian Wilson collaborator to transcribe (with full credit) some of the arrangements from his large collection of early *calypso* 78s. *Discover America,* which was originally released in 1972, is essentially a rock album, but a charming and eccentric one, even by the standards of its time; Parks' take on the composing and arranging of the *calypso* greats is accurate and revealing.

At its best, *soca* can be some of the most exciting dance music ever recorded. And far and away the best *soca* CD I have yet heard is Arrow's *O'La Soca* (Mango CCD 9835). The deliberate cheapness of the electronic effects in many *soca* releases can add to a sense of primitive, over-the- top fun—or it can make you wish you were listening to something else. But the production values for *O'La Soca* are never less than exquisite. The tracks are chock-full of interesting ideas, and Arrow is a strong and engaging singer whose energy never flags. The album contains a smoking version of the Neville Brothers' "Hey Pocky-Away" that includes a rap break that actually adds to the song's momentum, believe it or not. The title cut is an utter blast, both in the original that opens the album and the dub version that closes it. Of all the releases discussed in this book, *O'La Soca* is the one to buy first.

Any style as lyric-oriented as *soca* can be expected to have a political wing. And, whatever dilution of the groove that might entail, political texts in *soca* are quite popular, especially at the annual best-song competition in Trinidad's pre-Lent carnival. *When the Time Comes: Rebel Soca* (Shanachie CD 64010) documents this style ably, and the *soca* veteran Nelson's *When the World Turns Around* (Shanachie CD 64024) contains some powerful music. But the *soca* artist who comes closest to Bob Marley's genius for writing political/spiritual song lyrics that rise above the limitations of the form is Safi Abdullah.

Abdullah was born in Jamaica and, in the early sixties, played drums on many of the best *ska* records. When he moved to the United States to work with Eartha Kitt, he was drafted into the U.S. Army and sent to Vietnam. When he returned, he worked for several years with R&B groups like Archie Bell and the Drells and then studied music at the University of Dakar, Senegal, in West Africa. He began recording under his own

Safi Abdullah. *Courtesy Shanachie Records*

name in 1979, and his unique *soca/reggae/*funk style is best documented on *Another One Gone* (Shanachie CD 64023). Often fusions, even the most well-intended, can dissipate the rooted force of the musics involved. But in this case Safi Abdullah's personal vision is strong and unique enough to make it work. *Another One Gone* is a distinctive yet accessible piece of funky world-pop, passionately political and religious, comparable, in both its uplifting humanism and in Abdullah's ability to play many instruments well, to the best work of Stevie Wonder.

STEELBANDS

Another Trinidadian style enjoyed a certain vogue among American record-buyers a few decades back: the music of steelbands, large groups of musicians playing nothing but steel oil drums of various sizes, sawed in half and with the tops beaten into note-producing grids—a kind of homemade glockenspiel. Originally an adjunct to large criminal societies who would hold bloody streetfights each year at carnival time, the steelbands evolved into independent musical entities pursuing an entirely musical agenda with increasing sophistication.

This is another case in which a style has gone on developing after North American attention has waned. Most steelband records have gone out of print and few that remain are available on compact disc. One excellent collection is *The Heart of Steel: Steelbands of Trinidad and Tobago* (Flying Fish FF 70522). Although the liner notes are little more than a collection of black-nationalist slogans, this set was apparently recorded at one of the periodic competitions for island steelbands at Port of Spain, Trinidad. Some bands play music by Offenbach, Mendelssohn, or Tchaikovsky and others play original compositions, but all pieces are performed with fire and precision. The sound is good for what seems to be an outdoor recording.

DISCOGRAPHY

Bob Marley and the Wailers: *Catch a Fire* (Tuff Gong/Island 422-846201-2); *Burnin'* (Tuff Gong/Island 422-846200); *Natty Dread* (Tuff Gong/Island 422-846204-2); *Live* (Tuff Gong/Island 422-846203-2); **Survival* (Tuff Gong/Island 422-846202-2); and *Legend: The Best of Bob Marley and the Wailers* (Tuff Gong/Island 422-846210-2)

Peter Tosh: *Legalize It* (Columbia CK 34253) and *Equal Rights* (Columbia EK 34670)

Bunny Wailer: *Time Will Tell—A Tribute to Bob Marley* (Shanachie CD 43072)

Augustus Pablo: *Blowing with the Wind* (Shanachie CD 43076); *East of the River Nile* (Message CD 1003); and **Rockers Meets King Tubbys in a Fire House* (Shanachie CD 43001)

Towering Dub Inferno (Rykodisc RCD 20152)

Soundtrack: *The Harder They Come* (Mango CCD 9202)

Toots and the Maytals: *Funky Kingston* (Mango CCD 9330); **Reggae*

Got Soul (Mango CCD 9374); and *Toots in Memphis* (Mango CCD 9818)

Ras Michael: **Know Now* (Shanachie CD 64019); *Rally Round* (Shanachie CD 43027); and *Zion Train* (SST SSTCD 168)

Burning Spear: *Mek We Dweet* (Mango CCD 539863) and *Live In Paris* (Slash/Warner Brothers 25842-2)

Soundtrack: *Rockers* (Mango CCD 9587)

Alpha Blondy: *Jerusalem* (Shanachie CD 43054) and *The Best of Alpha Blondy* (Shanachie CD 43075)

Lucky Dube: *Prisoner* (Shanachie CD 43073) and *Slave* (Shanachie CD 43060)

More Intensified! Original Ska, Volume 2: 1963–1967 (Mango CCD 9597)

The Jolly Boys: *Pop 'N' Mento* (Rykodisc RCD 10185) and *Sunshine 'N' Water* (Rykodisc RCD 10187)

Gazoline: *Zouk Obsession* (Shanachie CD 64021)

***Konbit—Burning Rhythms of Haiti* (A&M 75021-5281-2)

Boukman Eksperyans: *Voudou Adjae* (Mango CCD 162-539-899)

A Carnival of Cuban Music Volume 1 (Rounder CD 5049)

A Carnival of Cuban Music Volume 2 (Rounder CD 5050)

Ruben Blades: *Buscando America* (Elektra 60352-2) and *Nothing but the Truth* (Elektra 60754-2)

Calypso Pioneers: 1912–1937 (Rounder CD 1039)

Calypso Breakaway: 1927–1941 (Rounder CD 1054-2)

Calypsos from Trinidad (Folklyric ARFL CD 7004)

Van Dyke Parks: *Discover America* (Warner Brothers 26145-2)

**Arrow: *O'La Soca* (Mango CCD 9835)

When the Time Comes: Rebel Soca (Shanachie CD 64010)

Nelson: *When the World Turns Around* (Shanachie CD 64024)

**Safi Abdullah: *Another One Gone* (Shanachie CD 64023)

***The Heart of Steel: Steelbands of Trinidad and Tobago* (Flying Fish FF 70522)

**Highly recommended

Clifton Chenier. *Photo by Howard Brainen, courtesy Arhoolie Records*

7
NORTH AMERICA

THE FIRST WORLD MUSIC was American music. The whole idea of combining various musics and cultures is uniquely American, rooted in our belief in the "melting pot." The first efforts to fuse the music of different communities into one style, the first use of recording technology to exchange music between communities, the first musics that were both widely popular and deeply rooted in the vernacular—all came from this continent.

As a nation of immigrants, we are a culture stitched together from many minority cultures. These minority groups had to interact—the material in the melting pot had to melt—or else the experiment would end in chaos. Music became the medium through which different cultures could experience each other at a distance. The gradual combination of musics (as in Texas, where the polka rhythms played by German settlers on accordion merged with the Spanish guitar songs of Mexico to make what is now called *conjunto* music) is a metaphor for the reconciliation of communities. It worked and, in working, changed the world.

It was a process that started with Edison's invention of the phonograph. Once people started buying phonographs, it was necessary that these phonographs have records to play. The businesses that sprang up to fill this need looked first, naturally enough, to the musics they heard in the urban, bourgeois environment they lived in: the music of the great European composers plus the show tunes and popular songs of the day. These last, as World War I ended, became flavored more and more with a new style of popular music called jazz, black-inflected improvisations from the streets and levees of polyglot New Orleans.

The jazz music of New Orleans was music very much of a time, a place, and a people. Through the twenties, as jazz came to dominate popular music the way rock does now, canny record-company executives began to look for other vernacular styles and discovered that recordings of rural singers and instrumentalists, especially from the South and Southwest, often sold very well both inside and outside of their respective communities. So, in hotel rooms and warehouses across the country, these companies recorded anybody they could find, at random, until the Great Depression forced them to retrench. Many of these recordings were a waste of wax, but some of them produced the greatest blues and country performers in history.

These recordings became a legacy left for a new generation of musicians who never would have known about the music otherwise. This generation of musicians used that legacy, and every other music they could wrap their chops around, to conquer the world via rock and roll in the 1950s. And it wasn't just rock and roll music that conquered the world; it was the *idea* of rock and roll—the idea that you could combine every music there was to combine and that out of it came a series of amazing, unknown hybrids. The noise that started in North America echoed back from successive receiving surfaces throughout the world: England in the sixties, Jamaica in the seventies, Africa in the eighties, and on into the future.

This book, as you know, deals with the echo, not the original explosion. But there have been some echoes here on this continent, as well as some vernacular musics whose development makes a statement about the place of subcultures in our society. And there are also some recordings that are included here out of simple personal bias, like the one we begin with.

THE HARLEM SPIRITUAL ENSEMBLE

It may be a stretch to include the devotional music of black Americans from the pre-Civil War period in a book about world music, especially considering that I had specifically said we would avoid gospel because it has too much to do, stylistically, with rock and roll. But the African chapters discuss hymn singers like Ladysmith Black Mambazo and Machanic Manyeruke and the Puritans, and nearly every other chapter deals with religious music of one kind or another, from the Rasta *reggae* of Jamaica to the Islamic *qawwali* singers of Pakistan.

The Harlem Spiritual Ensemble. *Courtesy Arcadia Records*

Harlem Spiritual Ensemble founder and music director Francois Clemmons (familiar to fans of the "Mr. Rogers' Neighborhood" television program) draws a distinction between spirituals and the more modern black-gospel sound, based mostly on gospel's use of instrumental accompaniment. On *The Harlem Spiritual Ensemble in Concert* (Arcadia ARC 1991-2) the six-member group, unamplified and accompanied only by occasional piano and hand-drum, makes a potent case for this nearly forgotten form.

Another authentic touch is the group's use of dialect, the broad vowels and swallowed consonants of old-time Southern speech giving the soaring melodies of pieces like "Go Down Moses" and "I've Been 'Buked" room to move. Clemmons is adamant about the importance of Southern dialect to this repertoire. Far from being a demeaning holdover from times now thankfully past, he sees it as the proper context in which this majestic music can flourish. From the evidence provided on this CD, this cultural heritage has a lot to say to all Americans today.

One high point of the CD is Clemmons's duet on "O! What a Beautiful City" with the group's cofounder, the extraordinary bass Louis Smart. Clemmons's tenor twines sinuously around Smart's deep bass, each verse-ending "Hallelooo . . ." held an extra measure for emphasis. Percussionist Morris McCormick provides the most interesting instrumental textures, subtly adding with his conga drum the Afro-Cuban accents Jelly Roll Morton called "the Spanish tinge." Other songs, like "Judas Was a Weak Man" and "I Wanna Be Ready," achieve a swaying, trancelike passion that, added to the fine singing and sure arrangements, communicates the deepest emotions of this most emotional of musics.

CAJUN AND ZYDECO

Probably the most prominent regional subculture in the United States at this time is found in the bayou country of

Louisiana and East Texas, where many French Canadians settled after the fall of Quebec to the British. The country they left behind them they called Acadia, and over time the self-appelation "Acadian" became "Cajun." These settlers were harmoniously joined in the 19th century by freed slaves, and the music of rural French-speaking Louisiana is now divided into two interdependent styles, based partly but not entirely on race. The "country" style is called Cajun music and features fiddle with accordion accompaniment, often with a triangle keeping the beat. The "rhythm and blues" style is called *zydeco,* from the patois pronunciation in the traditional song "Les Haricots N'ont pas Salé" or "There's No Salt in Your Snap Beans." In *zydeco,* the accordion is usually the lead instrument and the percussion is heavier, featuring a ridged metal "rubboard" worn on the chest and played with thimbles or metal bottle-openers. As both forms have become more popular, instrumentation has expanded: each style has seen a new generation of groups using drums, while *zydeco* artists have added horns and piano and Cajun groups have added electric and pedal steel guitars.

If Cajun still remains at times a subset of country music, complete with teary ballads about "notre divorce," and *zydeco* a subset of rhythm and blues, complete with lengthy exhortations to "boogie," the two styles appear to be growing closer together in recent years, meeting in a kind of bayou-rock middle ground in the work of artists like Zachary Richard (known as "the Cajun Bruce Springsteen"), Queen Ida, Beausoleil, and Buckwheat Zydeco. Cajun and *zydeco* have both gone through a number of generational changes already since the first records were made fifty years ago, because both styles assimilate outside influences voraciously.

CAJUN

Sometimes you just want the pure, unalloyed sound of traditional Cajun music. And *En Bas du Chene Vert* (Arhoolie CD

312) is as authentic an album as anyone could find, featuring the pre-eminent Cajun fiddler Dewey Balfa; Marc Savoy, builder of the Acadian accordion, the most highly prized accordion in Louisiana today; and D. L. Menard, author of several classic songs of the Cajun repertory. Recorded on November 13, 1976, *En Bas du Chene Vert* ("Under a Green Oak Tree") is first and foremost a showcase for Menard's singing, for which he has been called, with some justice, "the Cajun Hank Williams." But it also includes some of the finest playing of the mid-seventies Cajun revival.

Dewey Balfa, Marc Savoy, and D. L. Menard. *Courtesy Arhoolie Records*

As one of the culture's senior fiddlers, Dewey Balfa has perhaps done more over the last thirty years than anyone else to bring traditional Cajun music to the world. He is the only surviving member of the legendary Balfa Brothers, the first act from Cajun Louisiana to attract an audience among Northern folk-music enthusiasts. *The Balfa Brothers Play Traditional Cajun Music* (Swallow SW 6011) is the pre-eminent document of the group in the sixties and the definitive statement of the music as they played it. Another recording from this period is *J'ai Vu le Loup, le Renard, et la Belette* (Rounder CD 6007).

Chene Vert accordionist Marc Savoy has also been involved in a number of other traditionalist projects, all of them worth hearing. Especially worthy is the Savoy-Doucet Cajun Band, the trio he formed with his wife, Ann Savoy, and fiddler Michael Doucet, later of Beausoleil. One of this group's best outings is *Two-Step D'Amédé* (Arhoolie CD 316).

Of all the Cajun musicians yet mentioned, Michael Doucet may be the most universally familiar, through the growing international popularity of his group Beausoleil. Beausoleil's *Bayou Cadillac* (Rounder CD 6025) is a good example of the ways this expanded Cajun group (with trap drums, electric bass, electric guitars, and even saxophones augmenting the standard fiddle-accordion front line) incorporates *zydeco,* rock, jazz, and Caribbean music into the Cajun idiom. *Live! From the Left Coast* (Rounder CD 6035), recorded in San Francisco's Great American Music Hall, is a bit more straightforward in its pursuit of the Cajun-rock groove and, as such, it is a perfect party album. There are blues-flavored rhythmic grooves here, too, but always with the fiddle or accordion far enough forward to remind you what state the group comes from.

There are Beausoleil albums that are less ecumenical in their sources, although the group's musical curiosity is a great part of its charm. *Allons à Lafayette and More* (Arhoolie CD 308) features traditional fiddler Canray Fontenot, and *Déjà Vu* (Swallow SW 6080), culled from two early Beausoleil LPs and a couple of Michael Doucet's solo novelties, is also considerably smaller-scaled. Both of these are more fiddle with accompaniment than drums with fiddle lead, and there are a lot of old songs and fiddle tunes. *Déjà Vu* boasts "Arc d'Triumphe Two- Step" a solo novelty recorded on location in Paris in 1976 and "Love Bridge Waltz," recorded at President Carter's inaugural Folk-Ethnic Concert in 1977.

Doucet's brother David, guitarist for Beausoleil, has an album of his own that focuses on the guitar, an instrument whose role in Cajun music was almost nonexistent until the Cajun/country fusion of the early postwar years. *Quand J'ai*

Parti (Rounder CD 6040) has a lot of old tunes on it, led by Doucet's Doc Watson-style flatpicking and the bluesy dobro of longtime Roy Acuff sideman Oswald Kirby with the support of most of the members of Beausoleil.

The music's rock wing is led by Zachary Richard, whose part-*zydeco,* part-Cajun hybrid has won a fanatical following, especially in France and French Canada. *Women in the Room* (A&M 75021-5302-2), his major-label debut, takes that hybrid further, forsaking the usual drones in favor of a sharp, driving Cajun-rock. There is not much fiddle on this album and Richard's accordion is confined mostly to straightforward rock and roll keyboard vamps, reminiscent of Augie Meyer's organ fills on the early records of the Sir Douglas Quintet. Richard's most distinctive attribute, however, is his voice, by turns plaintive ("No French, No More") or hard-edged ("Who Stole My Monkey"). It is particularly affecting on "Manchac," a gripping ballad with a moody, atmospheric arrangement.

The feel of this varied album is relaxed—as befits a mobile studio parked in Scott, Louisiana—and five people are credited under the heading "culinary support," which carries a nice mental image of the musicians chowing down on catfish court bouillon between takes. But *Women in the Room* may be *too* varied for some tastes. As in many crossover bids, the eagerness to convey the breadth of a vernacular artist's talent can sacrifice a sense of continuity or context. The 1988 release *Zack's Bon Ton* (Rounder CD 6027), although it does not equal the high points of *Women in the Room,* is Richard's most consistent effort, and the favorite of his longtime fans.

Even closer to being real rock and roll bands, despite the use of the accordion as principal solo instrument, are Filé, whose *Cajun Dance Band* (Flying Fish FF 70418) is a dynamic slice of roadhouse dance music, and Wayne Toups and Zydecajun, whose name says everything needed about their musical intentions. But the common denominator of all Cajun and *zydeco* music is that people dance to it, whether it be old-time waltzes, country two-steps, or the boogaloo. And Zydecajun's

Blast from the Bayou (Mercury 836518) is eminently dance-able.

ZYDECO

The funkiest sound of all comes from the *zydeco* side of the tracks. *Zydeco* is like a fat man dancing the dirty boogie—it's not very subtle, but the house sure vibrates while it's going on. The instrument usually on top of the mix is a full-sized concert accordion (as opposed to the smaller, diatonic instruments played in most Cajun bands), and it is perfect for this music. Part organ, part harmonica, its asthmatic wheeze pushes the groove along like a bellows fanning a flame.

The undisputed king of *zydeco,* and one of its principal innovators, is the late Clifton Chenier. With his brother Cleveland on the rub-board and a crack blues band behind him, he never made a record that is not worth hearing, although some of his last recordings, made when he was ill, fall short of those made during his prime. His music did not change appreciably as he grew older and more successful, but given the many titles still in print, we will concentrate here on the early albums that helped him find a wider audience.

60 Minutes with the King of Zydeco (Arhoolie CD 301) is an excellent CD compilation taken from earlier LPs on the Arhoolie label, the company that did the most to make Chenier's reputation in the sixties. Other Arhoolie CDs include *Bogalusa Boogie* (Arhoolie CD 347), *King of Zydeco* (Arhoolie CD 355), and *Live at St. Mark's* (Arhoolie CD 313), a fine 1971 concert recording. In-concert albums played a large part in Chenier's recording career towards the end of his life. He developed a fanatical following in France, as might be expected, and *On Tour* (EPM FDC 5505), recorded live in France, is entertaining as much for the audience as anything else. *Bayou Blues* (Specialty SPCD 2139) is another early gem.

Unfortunately, Chenier died just as the vogue in all things Louisiana was beginning to peak, leaving the field he had cleared to be plowed and harvested by younger artists. His son, C. J. Chenier, and the Red-Hot Louisiana Band have begun to score with the brash, rocked-up style of *Hot Rod* (Slash 26263-2). And another hot young group is Buckwheat Zydeco (led by Stanley "Buckwheat" Dural, Jr.), whose CD *Where There's Smoke, There's Fire* (Island 422-842925-2) boasts guest appearances by several rock stars and even a promotional video shown on various music networks. An earlier, more rooted Buckwheat Zydeco CD is *Zydeco Party* (Rounder CD 11528), compiled from previous releases on the Rounder label.

Perhaps the most popular of the *zydeco*-roots groups is Queen Ida and the Bon Temps Zydeco Band, whose *On Tour* (GNP GNPD 2147) won a Grammy Award in 1982 for Best Ethnic Traditional Folk Album. Ida Guillory is an indefatigable singer, and the band knows its way around the *zydeco* groove without having to flirt too seriously with the vagaries of rhythm and blues. Rockin' Dopsie and the Twisters contributed a song to Paul Simon's *Graceland* album and have gone on to build a good-sized audience. *Saturday Night Zydeco* (Maison de Soul CD 104) is their best CD release. Terrance Simien and the Mallet Playboys are fairly new on the *zydeco* scene nationally, and their first release, *Zydeco on the Bayou* (Restless 72368-2), has some great moments.

But my favorite newcomer is actually a veteran, Boozoo Chavis. Chavis was making *zydeco* records in the forties, but it wasn't until the recent *Zydeco Trail Ride* (Maison de Soul CD 1034) that he began to shuck his reputation as a comic primitive and show himself as a real musician with an individual style that, while often eccentric (even surreal), has solid chops behind it. His repertoire of vocal inflections is, if not infinite, then certainly vast, a concatenation of grunts, snickers, heavy breathing, and animal sounds that can leave an audience dizzy with the sheer lunatic variety of it all.

FRENCH CANADIAN MUSIC

Of course, French culture remains strong in Canada, too. And La Bottine Souriant ("the Smiling Boot") is the most popular traditional group in French Canada. *Je Voudrais Changer D'Chapeau* (Rounder CD 6041), their seventh album and the first to be released in the United States, won a 1990 Juno Award (Canada's Grammy) for Best Folk Recording.

The folk-dance bands of Quebec, like their Cajun cousins in Louisiana, feature fiddle and accordion. But instead of the droning, bluesy quality of Cajun music, the Québecois bands favor sprightly, more chromatic tunes, with distinctive call-and-response harmonies sung heartily in unison. The modern touches La Bottine Souriant adds to its robust traditional roots are never overstated, from the the taped whale-song on "La Valse des Belugas" to the tasteful use of brass throughout. Anyone who liked the McGarrigle Sisters great 1980 LP *Frenchrecord* (not currently available on CD, alas!) will love *Je Voudrais Changer D'Chapeau*. Both are delightfully tuneful expressions of one of North America's most distinctive subcultures.

CONJUNTO AND MEXICAN MUSIC

Another area where two disparate musics formed into one, with equal input from both, is in the border regions of south Texas and northern Mexico. After the annexation of Texas in 1845, and through the post-Civil War years into the early 20th century, European immigrants (many of them German or Bohemian) settled in Texas, bringing their frolicsome polka music with them. What they found there was a vibrant Mexican culture that had remained more-or-less intact for the past 200 years, its own music based on romantic Spanish songs, often sung as tenor duets, and the *bajo sexto,* a kind of twelve-string guitar.

The southernmost counties in Texas remain overwhelmingly Mexican (in some towns persons of Mexican descent make up as much as eighty percent of the population), and a thriving Mexican dancehall scene on both sides of the Rio Grande features *conjuntos norteños* ("northern groups") that deftly combine the accordions and polkas of the immigrants with the song tradition and *bajo sextos* of the first settlers. In Texas the music is simply called *conjunto,* or sometimes "Tex-Mex," and most of these *conjunto* groups (like Denver's Table Mesa, the term "*conjunto* group" is something of a bilingual redundancy) are quartets: bass, drums, accordion, and *bajo sexto* or twelve-string. The accordion is the leading instrumental voice, and the greatest players (Flaco Jimenez, for example) are true virtuosi of the instrument.

After a period of decline in the sixties, during which the Mexican airwaves were glutted with the *mariachi* pop recently resurrected on Linda Ronstadt's recording *Canciones de mi Padre* (Asylum 60765-2), the more rooted sound of *conjunto* has slowly begun to reach a wider audience, both through the growing fame of individual musicians and the international visibility of San Antonio's annual Tejano Conjunto Festival. The response has been deservedly enthusiastic—*conjunto* at its best is wonderfully funky, a swinging dance music with a loose, first-take feel that, paradoxically, adds to the deep emotion of the singing.

The four-volume series *¡Conjunto!: Texas-Mexican Border Music* (*Volume 1,* Rounder CD 6023; *Volume 2,* Rounder CD 6024; *Volume 3,* Rounder CD 6030; *Volume 4,* Rounder CD 6034) licenses records from the various Texas and Mexican companies that service the *conjunto* market in the region, so they give a good indication of the authentic music in context. Another CD, compiled from the Mexican market, is Flaco Jimenez's *San Antonio Soul* (Rounder CD 6042), perhaps the best place to start for the extraordinary panharmonic accordion flights of this most famous of *conjunteros*. Another excellent source is *Ay Te Dejo en San Antonio* (Arhoolie CD 318), an hour-long collection of sessions from the early and middle eighties.

Los Pingüinos del Norte. *Courtesy Arhoolie Records*

Fred Zimmerle and Trio San Antonio.
Courtesy Arhoolie Records

Arhoolie Records is probably the leading company in the *conjunto* field today, at least so far as the wider national market is concerned. They have raided their copious vaults for hour-plus CD reissues of the many great *conjunto* artists they have recorded over the years, and many of these re-issues are excellent. Among them are *Conjuntos Norteños* (Arhoolie CD 311), a double album featuring Los Pingüinos del Norte ("the Penguins of the North") and Fred Zimmerle and Trio San Antonio. Recorded in an empty cantina across the river from

Eagle Pass, Texas, in the early seventies, *Conjuntos Norteños* has the earthy charm of unreconstructed roots music, especially the Trio San Antonio sides, featuring the impassioned singing of Fred Zimmerle. More modern releases include *The Many Sounds of Steve Jordan* (Arhoolie CD 319), an innovator in the use of accordion effects and fuller arrangements, and *El Mero, Mero de San Antonio* (Arhoolie CD 317) by Santiago Jimenez, Jr. The younger brother of Flaco, Jimenez has built up a loyal following through a rigorous national tour schedule.

Valerio Longoria. *Courtesy Arhoolie Records*

But my favorite *conjunto* recording of all is Valerio Longoria's *Caballo Viejo* (Arhoolie CD 336). Longoria, a pioneer accordionist since the forties, remains an expressive singer and magisterial bandleader to this day, and *Caballo Viejo* is the most varied and dynamic *conjunto* album I have heard. A questing musical intelligence, Longoria was responsible for bringing the *bolero* and *canción ranchera* styles into the music. More recently, he has drawn on Andean rhythms in his work: the *Peruviano* and especially the haunting minor-key *cumbias* of Colombia. And yet nothing sounds forced or out of context. Two sons and a grandson form his band, and their playing is of a musicality and grace found nowhere else.

There is quite a bit of *conjunto,* albeit Anglicized, in *Texas Tornados* (Reprise 26251-2), the first album by the all-star country-rock band of the same name. Freddy Fender, who got his start as the Mexican Elvis (universally known as "El Be-Bop"), and Doug Sahm and Augie Meyer, late of the beloved Sir Douglas Quintet, are joined by Flaco Jimenez in an entertaining collection of rock, country, and *conjunto* tunes.

The folk music of Mexico proper is given an engaging summary by the Mexican arts troupe Los Folkloristas in *¡Mexico!* (Flying Fish FF 70521), a province-by-province review of styles. Another take on Mexican folk comes from the Los Angeles rock band Los Lobos in *La Pistola y el Corazon* (Slash/Warner Brothers 25790-2), whose heartfelt singing and broad knowledge of the various forms belie the popular conception of rockers as antihistorical and subliterate.

HAWAIIAN MUSIC

With the explosion of tourism in Hawaii over the last fifty years or so, the distinctive traditions of Hawaiian music have become so watered down as to be almost faceless, an adjunct to the music of anonymous tourist lounges from Las Vegas to Sun City, South Africa. The original style, the dulcet *ukelele*-accompanied songs of the islands combined more recently with guitars imported by Portuguese cowboys and pineapple farmers (often played in the open-chord tunings known as "slack key" and often with a slide), lives on only in the work of a handful of revivalists and in recordings made as much as seventy years ago.

Most of the Hawaiian music listed in the *Schwann* catalogue, at least that falling within our purview, has yet to be released on CD, although things could change in the next few years. For now, the most exciting Hawaiian-music package available is the two-volume *Sol Hoopii—Master of*

Hawaiian Steel Guitar (*Volume 1,* Rounder CD 1024; *Volume 2,* Rounder CD 1025). Hoopii (the second syllable is accented) was the most famous Hawaiian musician of the twenties and thirties—the boom years of the Hawaiian music craze in this country. In 1919, he stowed away on a ship bound from his native Honolulu to San Francisco and supported himself in his first months in California as a prizefighter.

But his mastery of the slide guitar could not be ignored, and soon he was a prominent recording artist and a fixture in nightclubs, movies, and on national concert tours. His early records (represented on *Volume 1*) applied his precise touch and singing tone to jazz standards of the day like "St. Louis Blues" and "12th Street Rag," influencing future guitar stars like Roy Smeck and an entire generation of country and western players, many of whom made distinguished careers for themselves by playing his solos note for note. By 1930, Hoopii was making both jazz and more purely Hawaiian records, and in 1938 he renounced secular music, continuing to record and tour as an evangelist until his death in 1953. *Volume 2* includes these post-1930 records, some of them the brilliant "hot" jazz he was known for, some of them, equally brilliant, the sweetest of Hawaiian melodies. It also contains great, campy novelty songs like "Ten Little Toes" ("Ten little toes/One little nose/Are all I'm living for").

Two CDs document the best commercial recordings of the Hawaiian boom. *Vintage Hawaiian Music: The Great Singers, 1928–1934* (Rounder CD 1052) is an excellent compilation of traditional Hawaiian songs, and *Steel Guitar Masters, 1928–1934* (Rounder CD 1053) gives an overview of instrumental techniques. *Puerto Rican Music in Hawaii: Kachi-Kachi* (Smithsonian/Folkways CDSF 40014) is a more folkloric look at the cowboy music of the farming and ranching communities of the islands and its influence on the music as a whole. And the California rock guitarist Ry Cooder, an avid student of regional guitar styles, has recorded an album called *Chicken Skin Music* (Reprise 2254-2) with the slack-key guitar great

Gabby Pahinui. Until Pahinui's own albums are re-released, *Chicken Skin Music* (an Hawaiian slang phrase equivalent to "goosebumps") will do nicely. It is a charming and tuneful bit of revivalism.

MUSIC OF NATIVE AMERICANS

Many of the pre-Columbian cultures of North America were highly musical, and a lot of tribal songs have been recorded, both in the field as much as a hundred years ago and more recently by revivalists and other flame-keepers in those tribes remaining today. Although *Schwann* lists a number of LP releases, there are few compact discs available of Native American music, unfortunately.

One uplifting album of tribal songs is *Honor the Earth Powwow* (Rykodisc RCD 10199), recorded by Grateful Dead drummer Mickey Hart at a gathering of the Winnebago nation deep in the woods of northern Wisconsin and released as part of his series, "The World." *Honor the Earth Powwow,* like most American-Indian musics, is based on communal drumming rituals, with various tribal and family singing groups stepping forward to offer, over the drumbeat, songs for worship, dancing, or commemoration. These songs are part of a tradition that continues to produce new material; for instance, many songs written for ceremonies welcoming warriors back from battle have been updated to honor veterans of World War II and Vietnam.

The album is masterfully produced, as are all the albums in the series, and the music is varied and refreshing. Word has it that the Smithsonian Institution will be re-issuing some of the albums of American Indian music released on Folkways Records in the sixties, and those should reward the listener equally well.

DISCOGRAPHY

**The Harlem Spiritual Ensemble in Concert (Arcadia ARC 1991-2)

Dewey Balfa, Marc Savoy, and D. L. Menard: **En Bas du Chene Vert (Arhoolie CD 312)

The Balfa Brothers: **The Balfa Brothers Play Traditional Cajun Music** (Swallow SW 6011) and **J'ai Vu le Loup, le Renard, et la Belette** (Rounder CD 6007)

The Savoy-Doucet Cajun Band: **Two-Step D'Amédé** (Arhoolie CD 316)

Beausoleil: **Bayou Cadillac** (Rounder CD 6025); ****Live! from the Left Coast** (Rounder CD 6035); **Allons à Lafayette and More** (Arhoolie CD 308) with Canray Fontenot; and **Déjà Vu** (Swallow SW 6080)

David Doucet: **Quand J'ai Parti** (Rounder CD 6040)

Zachary Richard: **Women in the Room** (A&M 75021-5302-2) and **Zack's Bon Ton** (Rounder CD 6027)

Filé: **Cajun Dance Band** (Flying Fish FF 70418)

Wayne Toups and Zydecajun: **Blast from the Bayou** (Mercury 836518)

Clifton Chenier: ****60 Minutes with the King of Zydeco** (Arhoolie CD 301); **Bogalusa Boogie** (Arhoolie CD 347); **King of Zydeco** (Arhoolie CD 355); **Live at St. Mark's** (Arhoolie CD 313); **On Tour** (EPM FDC 5505); and **Bayou Blues** (Specialty SPCD 2139)

C. J. Chenier and the Red-Hot Louisiana Band: **Hot Rod** (Slash 26263-2)

Buckwheat Zydeco: **Where There's Smoke, There's Fire** (Island 422-842925-2) and **Zydeco Party** (Rounder CD 11528)

Queen Ida and the Bon Temps Zydeco Band: **On Tour** (GNP GNPD 2147)

Rockin' Dopsie and the Twisters: **Saturday Night Zydeco** (Maison de Soul CD 104)

Terrance Simien and the Mallet Playboys: **Zydeco on the Bayou** (Restless 72368-2)

Boozoo Chavis: **Zydeco Trail Ride** (Maison de Soul CD 1034)

La Bottine Souriant: **Je Voudrais Changer D'Chapeau (Rounder CD 6041)

Linda Ronstadt: **Canciones de mi Padre** (Asylum 60765-2)

¡Conjunto!: **Texas-Mexican Border Music** (**Volume 1,** Rounder CD 6023); ¡Conjunto!: **Texas-Mexican Border Music** (**Volume 2,** Rounder CD 6024); ¡Conjunto!: **Texas-Mexican Border Music**

(*Volume 3,* Rounder CD 6030); *¡Conjunto!: Texas-Mexican Border Music* (*Volume 4,* Rounder CD 6034)

Flaco Jimenez: *San Antonio Soul* (Rounder CD 6042) and *Ay Te Dejo en San Antonio* (Arhoolie CD 318)

Los Pingüinos del Norte/Fred Zimmerle and Trio San Antonio: *Conjuntos Norteños* (Arhoolie CD 311)

The Many Sounds of Steve Jordan (Arhoolie CD 319)

Santiago Jimenez, Jr.: *El Mero, Mero de San Antonio* (Arhoolie CD 317)

**Valerio Longoria: *Caballo Viejo* (Arhoolie CD 336)

The Texas Tornados (Reprise 26251-2)

Los Folkloristas: *¡Mexico!* (Flying Fish FF 70521)

Los Lobos: *La Pistola y el Corazon* (Slash/Warner Brothers 25790-2)

Sol Hoopii—Master of Hawaiian Steel Guitar Volume 1 (Rounder CD 1024) and **Sol Hoopii—Master of Hawaiian Steel Guitar Volume 2* (Rounder CD 1025)

Vintage Hawaiian Music: The Great Singers, 1928–1934 (Rounder CD 1052)

Steel Guitar Masters, 1928–1934 (Rounder CD 1053)

Puerto Rican Music in Hawaii: Kachi-Kachi (Smithsonian/Folkways CDSF 40014)

**Ry Cooder: *Chicken Skin Music* (Reprise 2254-2)

Honor the Earth Powwow (Rykodisc RCD 10199)

** Highly recommended

Margareth Menezes. *Courtesy Mango Records*

8

SOUTH AMERICA

WE HAVE DEALT WITH other regions for whom the world's perception of their popular music has been dominated by one particular country or style. But in South America this dominance—in this case by the music of Brazil—presents extra problems, because the music of Brazil has been a familiar part of American pop and jazz since the first records by *bossa nova* artists like Antonio Carlos Jobim and Astrud Gilberto were released in this country more than thirty years ago.

One is hamstrung by their success. The *bossa nova* beat can be found programmed in the rhythm attachments of even the cheapest electronic keyboards, and the lithe, smoky, understated timbres of Brazilian singers have become familiar enough that even the most debased cocktail-lounge soprano can recreate them with little or no strain. By the standard imposed in other chapters, most Brazilian musicians (with the possible exception of Afro-Brazilian artists from the Bahia province in the northeast) fall outside the boundaries of this survey. They're too familiar.

But it is such a terrific music: more sophisticated harmonically than any other style we funk-addled Westerners would call "danceable," carrying with it a subtle air of mystery and an understated sexual self-confidence that is instantly winning. But, while one can certainly tell the various stars of the music apart, the music is played at such a consistently high level that the question of which album one should buy becomes almost impossible to answer. The best place to start may be with compilations, so that listeners may hear several exponents of a given style and then look for individual albums by their favorites. And the fact is, although I have heard few if any Brazilian musicians who did not awaken in my breast the wildest enthusiasm, some compilations are better-programmed than others. That at least will give me a chance to avoid writing an endless, boring list of raves.

That said, we begin with a three-volume compilation that was something of a disappointment, the *Brazil Classics* series put together by David Byrne and Arto Lindsay: *Brazil Classics 1: Beleza Tropical* (Sire 25805-2); *Brazil Classics 2: O Samba* (Sire 26019-2); and *Brazil Classics 3: Forró, etc.* (Luaka Bop/ Warner Brothers 26323-2). Byrne, who for all his well-publicized interest in world music remains essentially a rock musician, could be expected to choose the most American-sounding selections he could find. But Lindsay, who has made probing, challenging music in his own right for many years and whose work as a producer for Brazilian pop singers like Marisa Monte shows both an understanding of the form and a willingness to take chances, might have been expected to come up with something a little less static.

The sampler that best conveys the breadth and vitality of true Brazilian pop is *Brazilliance: The Music of Rhythm* (Rykodisc RCD 20153). Although the grooves vary from the manic sprightliness of João Bosco's "Bala Com Bala" to the sinuous convolutions of Gal Costa's "Bem Bom" to the stately unfolding melody of "Estação Derradeira" by the great Chico Buarque, the album is essentially seamless, its twenty-two songs divided among only ten artists so that underlying themes and similarities can recur. But the main unifying factor among the songs on *Brazilliance* is the sheer quality of them all: each is a gem. I cannot recall another anthology that has so little filler material. Even among those CDs especially recommended, this one stands out.

A companion volume to *Brazilliance* is *Asa Branca: Accordion Forró from Brazil* (Rykodisc RCD 20154). *Forró,* with its roots in the farm country of the interior, is based on accordion and clarinet, echoing faintly the Boer "country" music of the South African veldt. But, being Brazilian, it cannot escape the swaying rhythms of the guitar, although it is calmer, simpler, and more homey than the fired-up *sambas* and majestic ballads of mainstream Brazilian pop. Another fine compilation of *forró* music is *Brazil—Forró (Music for Maids & Taxi Drivers)* (Rounder CD 5044).

THE BAHIA SCENE

There has been an intriguing transoceanic fusion going on in recent years in Brazil's Bahia province, the black-majority state at the country's northeast tip. The musical relationship between Bahia and the cosmopolitan cities of southern Brazil is roughly equivalent to the fifties and sixties in the United States, when black rhythm and blues artists came out of the rural south making music so much more rooted and moving than the prevailing showbiz acts of the North that it became known as "soul" music. Separated by the narrowest part of the Atlantic Ocean from the vibrant musical scene of West Africa—indeed, part of the same land mass a few ages ago—Bahian artists have become the "soul" singers of Brazil, reminding the culture of the emotional basis of the music and coming up with new approaches to its sources.

Margareth Menezes (pronounced "Mar-gar-RETCH Me-NEZ-isch") is a blunt, powerful singer with huge reserves of energy and a winning ability to lose herself in what she sings. Her knowledge of Afro-Brazilian music is comprehensive, but the songs on her album *Elegibo* (Mango CCD 539855-2) are not academic exercises or cultural overviews, just eloquent invitations to dance to some torrid polyrhythmic grooves.

A major star in her own country for several years, she had never been out of Brazil when David Byrne, of Talking Heads, invited her to New York in 1988 to join the world tour promoting his album of Latin music, *Rei Momo* (Sire 25990-2). She ended up singing in his band and performing a brief solo set that stole the show throughout North America, Europe, and Japan. The critical consensus at every stop was that Byrne had his work cut out for him just walking back out after she had finished. In the wake of this success, she recorded the duet "Dark Secret" with the Trinidadian singer David Rudder as part of the soundtrack for the film *Wild Orchid* starring Mickey Rourke and Jacqueline Bisset.

Another Bahian singer well worth hearing is Marisa Monte, both because her album *Mais* (World Pacific CDP 7-96104-2) takes some interesting stylistic liberties and because producer Arto Lindsay is able to re-establish himself as an exciting musical innovator thereby. The rhythms on *Mais* are more often defined by trap drums than on many Brazilian releases, giving it a flavor of American funk. This feeling is both reinforced and made more distinctive by periodic outbursts from Lindsay's buzz-saw electric guitar and the contributions of other American musicians like Marc Ribot and Bernie Worrell. Lindsay also skillfully factors in the saxophone squawks of fellow avant-downtown players Marty Ehrlich and John Zorn so that the dissonances do not intrude on the smoothness of the melodies but simply punctuate their most intense moments. The album is not all howling at the moon, however. Monte is a clear, expressive singer who has a way with a ballad, and *Mais* balances out into a fine piece of hemispheric pop.

There are plenty of other great singers and players from Bahia, and the best place to start checking them out is on *Axé Brazil: The Afro-Brazilian Music of Brazil* (World Pacific CDP

7-95057-2). *Axé* (pronounced "ah-shay") is nearly as compre-hensively entertaining as *Brazilliance,* with nineteen songs from eleven artists, many of them wonderful. Another Bahian specialty is *blocos,* large drum ensembles that play for the pre-Lenten Carneval. Paul Simon used one of the best *blocos* corps, Olodum, on the song "The Obvious Child" from his album *The Rhythm of the Saints* (Warner Brothers 26091-2) and in the concert tour that followed. The best compilation of *blocos* music is *Bloco Afro: Beats of Bahia* (Intuition C21S 91652), with Olodum, Ara Ketu, and other *blocos* ensembles, recorded during Carneval in Bahia, 1988 and 1989. There is something of the Mardi Gras parades of New Orleans in this music and something of the steelband music of Trinidad, al-though without the melodic depth of tuned percussion. But the rhythms will have you up and marching around the room.

OTHER SOUTH AMERICAN SOUNDS

The problem with the music of the rest of South America is not that it is not in print, it's just that almost all releases are either wildly esoteric, like the many recordings of the Andean harp or panpipes, and thus impossible to tell apart from each other in any sort of meaningful way from a North American perspective, or else they document popular music styles that have not altered much in their interaction with the music of the outside world, like the Argentine tango.

A few releases bear repeated listening. *Fiesta Vallenata* (Shanachie CD 64014) is more or less the soundtrack of *Shot-guns and Accordions: Music from the Marijuana-Growing Regions of Colombia,* one of the *Beats of the Heart* home video series. At first hearing, the *Vallenata* style of northern, Atlan-tic-coast Colombia has a lot in common with the *conjunto* music of south Texas: small groups fronted by accordion with tenor-duet vocals. But the comparison does not hold up. *Val-lenata* rhythms are more sprightly—less driving than in *con-junto*—and the accompaniment is looser. Percussion comes

Fiesta Vallenata. *Courtesy Shanachie Records*

from a collection of hand-drums, rattles, and shakers, and the bass is played in astonishing counterpoint to the prevailing rhythms, functioning less as accompaniment on the bottom, less even as "lead bass" in the sense that certain American funk and jazz players use it, than as another percussion instrument, responsible for the outermost polyrhythms conceivable. It makes for a light-hearted, even tipsy combination that may not be danceable in the James Brown sense, but is certainly danceable in the Charlie Chaplin sense.

Danceable in a sense only known by those who play it is the *huayno* (pronounced "wino") music of the Peruvian Andes. Using fiddle, harp, mandolin, accordion, saxophone, flute, or guitar in any of an infinite number of combinations, Peruvian hillbillies of both Incan and Spanish descent have put together this distinctly spacey amalgam of folk and popular styles that probably sounds truly majestic once you get above the tree line but at any altitude has a wacky charm. *Huayno: Music of Peru, Volume 1 (1949–1989)* (Arhoolie CD 320) is an hour's worth of the most popular recordings of the last forty years, taken from the vaults of various Peruvian record companies. There is enough music here that the listener can select the pieces he or she likes, program the rest out, and still enjoy this oddly haunting music. A more folkloric look at the music of various Andean countries is Sukay's *Instrumental Music of the Andes* (Flying Fish FF 70108).

DISCOGRAPHY

Brazil Classics 1: Beleza Tropical (Sire 25805-2)
Brazil Classics 2: O Samba (Sire 26019-2)
Brazil Classics 3: Forró, etc. (Luaka Bop/Warner Brothers 26323-2)
**Brazilliance: The Music of Rhythm* (Rykodisc RCD 20153)
Asa Branca: Accordion Forró from Brazil (Rykodisc RCD 20154)
Brazil—Forró (Music for Maids & Taxi Drivers) (Rounder CD 5044)
Margareth Menezes: *Elegibo* (Mango CCD 539855-2)
David Byrne: *Rei Momo* (Sire 25990-2)
**Marisa Monte: *Mais* (World Pacific CDP 7-96104-2)
**Axé Brazil: The Afro-Brazilian Music of Brazil* (World Pacific CDP 7-95057-2)
Paul Simon: *The Rhythm of the Saints* (Warner Brothers 26091-2)
Bloco Afro: Beats of Bahia (Intuition C21S 91652)
**Fiesta Vallenata: Hot Pop from Colombia* (Shanachie CD 64014)
Huayno: Music of Peru, Volume 1 (1949–1989) (Arhoolie CD 320)
Sukay: *Instrumental Music of the Andes* (Flying Fish FF 70108)

** Highly recommended

Shobha Gurtu. *Courtesy CMP Records*

9

~~~~~~~~~~~~~~

INDIA AND
AUSTRALASIA

IT DOESN'T MAKE A lot of sense to combine India with Australasia in this one skinny chapter, but the fact is that the majority of releases from these regions fall outside the bounds of this survey. Most of what people usually consider "Indian" albums feature "classical" music (a point that *raga*-masters like Ravi Shankar make continually), which is to say a court music made by a virtuoso class in the context of the specific formal dictates of the style. There is such a thing as Indian popular music, but the Indian entertainment industry, the largest in the world, has codified and standardized it to such an extent that few if any releases would hold the interest of listeners with a taste for the genre-bending artists of other cultures.

Now, to say that there is no genre-bending in Indian music would be to commit a schoolboy howler of the highest magnitude; but the technical virtuosity and harmonic sophistication involved in Indian music generally tends to lead its ex-

133

perimentalists into jazz. The Indian influence in jazz has been profound and beneficial over the last thirty years or more but, as I said in the Introduction, this book is not about jazz, and my call as to whether a world-fusion album is "too jazzy" is a judgment call the reader will simply have to live with. And if there are some commonly used Indian scales that bring to my mind nothing so much as "Boris the Spider" by the Who, I know that is nobody's fault but mine but, then again, it's my book.

The addition of Australasia makes this chapter something of a grab bag, but the music of Asia (and most notably Japan) is similar to that of the subcontinent in that the roots of the various musics are by and large "classical" and that most stylistic experiments end up in the jazz or new-age bins. And native Australian music is for the most part confined either to aboriginal field-recordings of largely anthropological interest or to guitar-strumming white left-wingers of a sort that has become all too familiar in this country already.

SUFI/ISLAMIC MUSIC

Qawwali is the devotional singing of the Sufi sect of Islam. According to legend, it began in the 12th century, when the Sufi saint Hazrat Moinuddin Chisti first began evangelizing among the Hindus of the subcontinent. Hindu devotional music was so beautiful that he realized the way to their hearts was to sing, not speak, the praises of Allah. The resulting music is ecstatic and mystical, drawing on ancient Turko-Persian poetry in which the language of the senses is used as an extended allegory, thus, "the Beloved" is God, "wine" is the knowledge and love of God, "the Tavern" is the heart, and physical beauty is analogous to illumination.

This deeply emotional singing, by turns raucous and serene, is a series of improvised variations on traditional themes. Singers are usually accompanied on harmonium, with a chorus and *tabla* drummers. There is a strong connection between *qawwali* and the gospel music of American blacks: the repetitions of a phrase building through a series of subtle changes, the sheer length of the performances and their cathartic expressiveness, and the sense that singing is itself a form of worship.

Nusrat Fateh Ali Khan. *Courtesy Shanachie Records*

Three CDs show *qawwali* singing to its best advantage: *Ya Habib* (Virgin/RealWorld 91346-2) by the Sabri Brothers, and two by the great Nusrat Fateh Ali Khan: *The Day, the Night, the Dawn, the Dusk* (Shanachie CD 64032) and *Shahen Shah* (Virgin/RealWorld 91300-2). The Sabri Brothers feature several harmoniums and a good-sized chorus, while *The Day, the Night, the Dawn, the Dusk* emphasizes Khan's voice in more intimate settings. On both albums, sixty minutes or more of playing time are devoted to three songs, so it takes a while for the performances to catch fire, but it is well worth the wait. Khan in particular gets in some unbelievable phrases, although his single best recorded performance is on the sampler album *The Compact RealWorld* (Virgin/RealWorld 91355-2).

INDIA/AMERICA FUSIONS

One tends to recoil from albums whose liner notes contain phrases like "When I first travelled to India I was overwhelmed by an incredible variety of experiences." But the album on which this phrase occurs, Jai Uttal's *Footprints* (Triloka 183-2), is no hippie half-fare excursion. It's a serious and eminently listenable fusion of Eastern musical forms with American rhythms and advanced studio technology.

Roger Nichols, engineer on all of Steely Dan's great jazz-rock records of the 1970s, is listed as "Production Consultant" in the credits, and *Footprints* has some of the advanced harmonic sense of Dan albums like *Aja*. Uttal plays most of the instruments here, including the guitar-like *dotar,* assorted percussion, and some intriguing samples of native sounds like the flutes used by snake charmers. Jazz trumpeter Don Cherry (also featured on *Mandingo Griot Society,* one of my favorite West African releases) plays some piquant solos on pocket trumpet, and Lakshmi Shankar sings a beautiful duet with Uttal on "Raghupati." The entire production is a delight, free of the devotional excesses of so many Indiaphiles and free also from an over-intellectual jazz approach.

Another fusion of Indian and American music comes from Ashwin Batish, founder of the Batish Institute, an Indian-music school and publishing house in Santa Clara, California. His *Sitar Power* (Shanachie CD 64004) is a somewhat less-sophisticated attempt to graft dance rhythms onto *raga*-influenced tracks. The *sitar* playing is often fine, but the album's production values are not up to the standards set by *Footprints*. The Institute does offer its own line of recordings on cassette, and fans of Indian folk, classical, and fusion music should send for a catalogue (see Appendix A for the address).

Najma. *Photo by Tom Boulting, courtesy Shanachie Records*

But the most successful Indian folk/funk/classical fusion is *Atish* (Shanachie CD 64026), a back-to-the-roots effort by the Indian pop diva Najma. Najma had the sense not to go completely folk on this album, but instead carefully layers electronic drums in among the *tablas,* discreetly alters her singing in spots through the judicious application of modern studio techniques, and gives most instrumental solos to a Western instrument, the soprano saxophone.

At their best, and they are rarely far from their best, the grooves are subtle and hypnotic, danceable in a sense not usually found in even the most rhythmic Indian music, but always rooted enough that one never doubts the musicians know exactly where the music is coming from. And Najma's singing is always gorgeous—a combination, again, of strictly Indian timbres with a more universal sense of swing that gives her voice a powerful allure. It is music from an Orientalist poet's most perfumed dreams, the heavenly sprite hovering just out of reach, singing to one's own ears a hymn of bliss, but funky.

A more traditional Indian soprano is heard on *Shoba Gurtu* (CMP CMPCD 3004), a self-named album from the Indian film-score singer and mother of jazz-fusionist *tabla* drummer Trilok Gurtu. Accompanied only by harmonium, *tabla,* and *sarangi,* the bowed lyre of the northern provinces, Gurtu sings in a number of light-classical and *raga* styles with an expressiveness born of long experience. In considering this recording we may be venturing too close to "official" Indian music, but the rewards are worth the risk.

AUSTRALIA

A traditional instrument of the aborigines of northern Australia, the *didgeridoo* is made from a tree trunk five or six feet long and up to six inches in diameter, left hollow by termites. Essentially a one-note drone instrument, it is played by blowing in one end and buzzing the lips to exploit the resonances and harmonics of the chamber. It has attained a certain vogue among exoticists of the world-music community, especially in Europe, but until now no one has really found a context in which it can relate to any other music of the world besides its own.

Outback, an English instrumental duo featuring Martin Craddick on guitar and mandolin and Graham Wiggins on the *didgeridoo,* seems to have managed it. On *Baka* (Hannibal HNCD 1357) Craddick's guitar playing is accomplished and diverse, but the *didgeridoo* more than keeps pace. It is, in fact, the center of the music in many ways, despite its lack of chromaticism. Wiggins uses it as a kind of blown percussion instrument, driving the songs with a large vocabulary of flatulent honks, buzzes, and hums. Despite the fact that they can only play in one key, Outback's songs are each distinct and memorable, with strong melodies and an eerie, otherworldly power.

ASIA

Another album that, like *Shoba Gurtu,* edges fairly close to "official" music but is worth considering for a number of reasons, is the Gyuto Monks' *Freedom Chants from the Roof of the World* (Rykodisc RCD 20113). Produced by Mickey Hart as part of his "The World" series, *Freedom Chants* achieved a larger success than most albums of this type, partly because of its stellar production values, partly because many American Buddhists found it to be an aid to meditation, and partly as a gesture of solidarity to the Tibetan people, victims of a brutal occupation by the People's Republic of China that has forced the country's spiritual leader, the Dalai Lama, into exile.

The Gyuto Monks chant mostly in unison, with some contrapuntal lines, using a deep, chiming bass-falsetto whose harmonics produce in the choir's leading singers as many as three notes at a time. Some of the chants are unaccompanied, while others include various Tibetan horns and drums. It is not the easy, flowing music that Westerners have come to associate with meditation, but its rigorous, sturdy spirituality can be bracing for those whose religion runs deep enough. Another CD by the Gyuto Monks is *Gyuto Tantric Choir* (Windham Hill WD 2001).

In part because of the Chinese occupation of Tibet and in part because of the T'ien An Men Square massacre and subsequent human-rights abuses in mainland China, Chinese music as a whole has become difficult for many people to enjoy, unfortunately. Many Western compilations recorded after the normalization of relations in the 1970s, such as *Music from the People's Republic of China* (Rounder CD 4008), are the work of starry-eyed American leftists, whose gee-whiz approach seems less appropriate these days.

One valuable release comes from the Guo Brothers, who were brought to London by David Byrne to help score the film *The Last Emperor* and have lived there since as exiles. Their album *Yuan* (Virgin/RealWorld 91345-2) is a modern pastiche of Chinese flutes, viols, and bells, with the discriminating addition of synthesizer in a few places.

The Korean percussion ensemble Samul-Nori has created a heady concoction with their *Music for Drums and Voices* (CMP CMPCD 3002) album. Reminiscent in its melodic approach to the group-percussion of albums produced by Mickey Hart for the West African master drummer Olatunji, *Music for Drums and Voices* explores a number of distinctive and entertaining grooves, combining rootsy high spirits with masterful control.

The Asian album that most successfully resists all categorization is *The New International Trio* (Flying Fish/Atomic Theory ATD 1102). This Cambodian-American group combines dozens of instruments from Southeast Asia with European baroque instruments like the virginal, fiddles and bagpipes from all over the world, and a jazzy clarinet to produce music that, amazingly, carries with it a strong sense of place. It is as if after a State Department-sponsored concert by a jazz group and a classical ensemble before the imperial court of Cambodia, the various American musicians dug up every local virtuoso they could find and held a huge jam session, covering material from every tradition imaginable, yet perfectly rehearsed and well thought out. Somehow it all works.

An Asian group that has found considerable acceptance in this country is Kodo, a communal company of improvisers from Japan specializing in traditional Japanese *daiko* drums, among other instruments. Their *Heartbeat Drummers of Japan* (Sheffield Lab CD KODO) contains no dead spots and plenty of surprises.

Central to the group's music are the four sizes of *daiko* drum: the *shime-daiko,* a roped drum comparable in size to the

Kodo. *Courtesy Dennis Letzler Organization*

Western snare drum; the *oke-daiko,* carried over the shoulder or played on a stand; the *miya-daiko,* too large to be carried, played with sticks the size of rolling pins; and, finally, the massive *O-daiko,* carved from a single tree trunk, measuring five feet across and weighing 800 pounds. Kodo intersperses numbers featuring these drums, in various combinations, with pieces for wooden flute, three-stringed *samisen,* gongs, small hand cymbals called *chappa,* and *gamelan,* bell-like metal bars struck with mallets.

All the drums are tuned with a precision that enables the players to calibrate their rhythms and dynamics exactly. Unison figures are astonishingly tight and crescendos and decrescendos seem to come from out of nowhere, producing some startling timbral effects. The massed *shime-daiko* produce sheets of pure sound, seemingly unrelated to individual notes struck by individual sticks. In several pieces where a lead drum plays variations over a set rhythm, the effect is more textural than musical, the tones sounding almost synthesized.

Occasional passages remind one of Western drummers. The *chappa* cymbals often bear an uncanny resemblance to the work of Zutty Singleton, drummer on some of the pioneering recordings of Louis Armstrong in the 1920s. And some of the ensemble pieces for *oke-daiko* and *miya-daiko* sound like noth-

nothing so much as the great British drummer Ginger Baker's solos on double-bass drumkit with the legendary rock band Cream.

DISCOGRAPHY

**The Sabri Brothers: *Ya Habib* (Virgin/RealWorld 91346-2)

Nusrat Fateh Ali Khan: *The Day, the Night, the Dawn, the Dusk* (Shanachie CD 64032) and *Shahen Shah* (Virgin/RealWorld 91300-2)

The Compact RealWorld (Virgin/RealWorld 91355-2)

Jai Uttal: *Footprints* (Triloka 183-2)

Ashwin Batish: *Sitar Power* (Shanachie CD 64004)

**Najma: *Atish* (Shanachie CD 64026)

Shoba Gurtu (CMP CMPCD 3004)

**Outback: *Baka* (Hannibal HNCD 1357)

The Gyuto Monks: *Freedom Chants from the Roof of the World* (Rykodisc RCD 20113) and *Gyuto Tantric Choir* (Windham Hill WD 2001)

Music from the People's Republic of China (Rounder CD 4008)

The Guo Brothers: *Yuan* (Virgin/RealWorld 91345-2)

Samul-Nori: *Music for Drums and Voices* (CMP CMPCD 3002)

***The New International Trio* (Flying Fish/Atomic Theory ATD 1102)

Kodo: *Heartbeat Drummers of Japan* (Sheffield Lab CD KODO)

**Highly recommended

Afterword

IF I HAD TO guess, I would say that everyone will have a favorite performer they think should have been included here that has not been. I apologize both for and to those who I may have left out, and can excuse myself by saying again that this is not an encyclopaedia, but a personal, and even eccentric, vision of the music of the world and some releases that will please those interested in listening to more of it.

At the beginning of this project I wondered what I would do about those releases that were impossible to categorize. With my usual arrogance, I decided that all albums could be categorized, at least roughly enough to fit into the regional format I chose for the book. There has been only one exception, really. That is the vastly entertaining Fuse: World Dance Music (4th & Broadway 444024-2), a sampler of various house-music mixes from Indian and North African producers centered in London.

House is the synthesized, psychedelic-flavored disco popular in Europe beginning in the late eighties and becoming more popular here as time goes by. As such, *Fuse* would be just another Anglo-American dance-pop exercise except that these producers are incorporating samples of world music in their mixes. These samples—including snatches of Afro-American chain-gang singing, flamenco guitar, Japanese flutes, Muslim chanting, and several different Indian instruments and drums—are sometimes altered in the studio, sometimes played straight. Then they are combined with the thumping, buzzing rhythm tracks of house to make fascinating, witty dance music filled with bizarre and interesting touches.

Many of the cuts were produced by Talvin Singh or Harri Kakouli under various interchangeable group identities such as Sapna, Paradise, and Mahatma T. These records often feature samples of Indian instruments, drums, or singing in various combinations with James Brown-style rhythms. "Shanti" by Mahatma T. even sounds a little like "What's Going On"-era Marvin Gaye with its impassioned vocals from Jon S. On other cuts, producer David Harrow specializes in samples from Islamic dance music, especially in Pulse 8's "Radio Morocco," featuring Jah Wobble, late of the seminal postpunk band Public Image Ltd.

The fact is that the individual tracks that make up these songs come from all over the map, making it quite impossible to pin down, or even approximate, what region any given song belongs to. One hesitates to make large "the future of world music" predictions, partly because such statements serve no useful purpose to a book like this one and partly because one is too busy dancing. These trippy, innovative mixes manage to be both excruciatingly hip and enjoyable, which is no small accomplishment.

But whether this is the future of world music or not, it is a nice note to go out on, the little voice with the funny accent on "Radio Morocco" chanting through reams of static, seemingly across a vast desert of misunderstanding and distrust, the simple message of the heartbeat we all dance to—"Funky people/Funky people/Funky people/'Allo?/'Allo?/Raddio Marrakech?"

Appendix A

MAIL-ORDER ADDRESSES

MOST OF THE CDs discussed in this volume are the products of independent record labels. That is not surprising. Independent labels have led the recording industry into many of the most challenging musics in our history, ever since the birth of the technology. Distribution of independent labels, however, can be a patchwork affair. Thus, in an attempt to reach as many customers as possible, most of these labels augment their sales in the better class of record stores with direct catalogue mail orders originating from their own warehouses.

All these companies will state, however, that they would prefer potential customers to look for their product in retail stores first, using mail order as a last resort. Retail sales are the backbone of any record company, and independent labels, in particular, are anxious to develop ties to as many retail stores and chains as possible. If enough people ask for a given release, even the most pop-oriented operation will give in to self-interest and stock that release. Further, most record stores can special-order any album currently in print, and some can get imports as well.

Down Home Music is one of the largest specialty mail-order houses in the world and their catalogue is filled with blues, old-time country, folk, jazz, Cajun, *zydeco,* western swing, Tex-Mex, *calypso, klezmer,* gospel, and vernacular music of all kinds from most of the greatest record companies known to man. They also carry a large selection of books, magazines, and videos.

Down Home Music
6921 Stockton Avenue
El Cerrito, CA 94530
510-525-1494
510-525-2904 (fax)

Catalogues are also available from the following record companies whose products are listed in this book. Those listed with an asterisk also carry records on other labels.

A&M
1416 North La Brea Avenue
Los Angeles, CA 90028

Allegro Imports
3434 SE Milwaukee Avenue
Portland, OR 97202
503-232-4213

Arcadia Records
4-10 West 101st Street, Suite 35
New York, NY 10025
212-749-3657

Arhoolie Records
10341 San Pablo Avenue
El Cerrito, CA 94530
415-525-7471

Asylum. *See* Elektra/Nonesuch.

Atoll. *See* Allegro Imports.

Axiom. *See* Island Records.

Batish Institute of Music
1316 Mission Street
Santa Cruz, CA 95060
408-423-1699
(Batish Institute of Music is a small company specializing in progressive Indian music and Indian fusions.)

Capitol Records, Inc.
1750 North Vine Street
Hollywood, CA 90028
213-462-6252

Celluloid Records
330 Hudson Street
New York, NY 10013
212-741-8310

CMP Records
155 West 72nd Street, Suite 706
New York, NY 10023
212-769-9362

Columbia Records
Sony Music Distribution
PO Box 4450
New York, NY 10101

Dorian Recordings
17 State Street, Suite 2E
Troy, NY 12180
518-774-5475

Elektra/Nonesuch
75 Rockefeller Plaza
New York, NY 10019

EPM. *See* Qualiton Imports.

Fantasy Records
10th and Parker
Berkeley, CA 94710
415-549-2500

Flying Fish Records
1304 West Schubert
Chicago, IL 60614
312-528-5455

Folklyric. *See* Arhoolie Records.

Fontana
c/o Polygram Group Distribution
Worldwide Plaza
825 8th Avenue
New York, NY 10019
212-333-8000

4th and Broadway. *See* Island Records.

Gallo. *See* Qualiton Imports.

GNP
8400 Sunset Boulevard
Los Angeles, CA 90069

Green Linnet Records
43 Beaver Brook Road
Danbury, CT 06810
203-730-0333

Hannibal Records. *See* Rykodisc.

Intuition. *See* Capitol Records, Inc.

Island Records
14 East 4th Street
New York, NY 10012
212-995-7800

JVC. *See* Allegro Imports.

Maison de Soul Records. *See* Swallow.

Mango Records. *See* Island Records.

Message Records
c/o Koch International
2700 Shames Dr.
Westbury, NY 11590
516-333-4800

Music of the World
PO Box 3620
Chapel Hill, NC 27515

Qualiton Imports
24-02 40th Avenue
Long Island City, NY 11101
718-937-8515

Reprise. *See* Warner Brothers Records.

Restless Records
11264 Plaza Court
Culver City, CA 90231
213-390-9969

Rhythm Safari (a division of H.R. Music)
5430 Van Nuys Boulevard, Suite 305
Van Nuys, CA 91401

*Rounder Records
One Camp Street
Cambridge, MA 02140
617-354-0700

Run River
c/o Goldcastle Records
3575 Cahuenga Blvd. W., Suite 470
Los Angeles, CA 90068
213-850-3321

Rykodisc
Pickering Wharf
Building C-3G
Salem, MA 01970
508-744-7678

*Shanachie Records
PO Box 208
Newton, NJ 07860
201-579-7763
201-579-7083 (fax)

Sheffield Lab
Box 5332
Santa Barbara, CA 93108
800-235-5737

Sire. *See* Warner Brothers Records.

Slash. *See* Warner Brothers Records.

Smithsonian/Folkways. *See* Rounder Records.

Specialty. *See* Fantasy Records.

SST Records
PO Box 1
Lawndale, CA 90260
213-430-7687

*Swallow
Distributed by Flat Town Music Co.
Drawer 10
Ville Platte, LA 70586
318-363-2184

(Floyd Soileau's Cajun label Swallow and its *zydeco* cousin Maison de Soul seem to release albums by every performer in southwest Louisiana and east Texas. It's kind of a Mom-and-Pop operation, so not many of their releases are going to be on CD, but it's a worthwhile catalogue to get if you are serious about Louisiana music. Besides, it's the only place I know of that sells plastic crawfish earrings through the mail.)

Temple. *See* Flying Fish Records.

Triloka
1001 North Poinsetta Place
West Hollywood, CA 90046
213-850-0806

Warner Brothers Records
3300 Warner Boulevard
Burbank, CA 91510

World Pacific. *See* Capitol Records, Inc.

Appendix B

RETAIL RECORD STORES

AS I HAVE MADE plain, this volume does not list every world-music CD available in this country. Even if it did, the curious reader would not find any mention of the many fine CDs that have not been released here but are available as imports. Besides, the analog-minded may even want cassettes or LPs.

Record stores that feature world music usually have an evangelical streak—the people who run the stores love the music themselves and want you to know about it. So browsing and asking dumb questions can be a great way to find more great releases. Here is a list of retail record stores that stock a lot of our favorite stuff. An afternoon spent prowling the record-store aisles in almost any town should yield at least some worthwhile world music. Support your local retailer!

Tower Records
(*Look in the "International" section. Locations in New York, San Francisco, Los Angeles, and other major cities.*)

ALASKA

Metro Books and Records
530 Spenard Road
Anchorage, AK 99503

CALIFORNIA

Leopold's
2518 Durant Avenue
Berkeley, CA 94704

Trade Roots Records
4799 Voltaire
San Diego, CA 92107

Round World Music
1491A Guerrero Street
San Francisco, CA 94110

Cymbaline
435 Front Street
Santa Cruz, CA 95060

Rhino Records
1720 Westwood Boulevard
Westwood, CA 90024

COLORADO

The Malt Shop
6231 East 14th Street
Denver, CO 80220

DISTRICT OF COLUMBIA

African Music Gallery
1352 U Street NW
Washington, DC 20009

Kilimanjaro International Records
1781 Florida Avenue NW
Washington, DC 20009

FLORIDA

Les Cousins
7858 NE 2nd Avenue
Miami, FL 33138
(*Haitian music*)

Peaches Records
2798 East Fowler Avenue
Tampa, FL 33612

HAWAII

Jelly's Comics & Books
Pearl Kai Shopping Center
Aiea, HI 96701

ILLINOIS

Record Service
621 East Green
Champaign, IL 61801

Record Swap
606½ East Green
Champaign, IL 61801

Rose Records
(*several locations in Chicago*)

Vintage Vinyl
6 B Nameoki
Granite, IL 62040

MASSACHUSETTS

Nuggets
482 Commonwealth Avenue
Boston, MA 02215

Cheapo Records
645 Massachusetts Avenue
Cambridge, MA 02139

MICHIGAN

Schoolkid's Records
523 East Liberty
Ann Arbor, MI 48104

Sam's Jams
279 West Nine Mile Road
Ferndale, MI 48220

MINNESOTA

Electric Fetus
2010 4th Avenue South
Minneapolis, MN 55404

MISSOURI

Streetside Records
6314 Delmar Boulevard
St. Louis, MO 63130

West End Wax
389 North Euclid Avenue
St. Louis, MO 63108

Vintage Vinyl
6362 Delmar Boulevard
University City, MO 65767
(*Give my love to Tom and Lew.*)

NEW HAMPSHIRE

The Dartmouth Bookstore
33 South Main
Hanover, NH 03655
(*will special order*)

NEW JERSEY

Princeton Record Exchange
20 Tulane Street
Princeton, NJ 08542

NEW YORK

Charlie's
1273 Fulton Street
Brooklyn, NY 11238
(*The nerve center for Brooklyn's Caribbean community—
lots of soca.*)

Baté
140 Delancy Street
New York, NY 10002
(*Latin music*)

Casa Latina
116th and Lexington
New York, NY 10029
(*Latin specialists*)

Center for Cuban Studies
124 West 23rd Street
New York, NY 10011
(*Cuban imports*)

HMV (2 locations)
2081 Broadway (and 72nd)
1280 Lexington Avenue (and 86th)
New York, NY 10023

Record Mart
Times Square Subway Station
New York, NY 10036
(*Good for Latin music, ask for Harry.*)

Shikhulu Records
274 West 125th Street
New York, NY 10027
(*lots of African imports*)

OREGON

Balladeer Music
296 East 5th Avenue
Eugene, OR 97401

Artichoke Music
3522S East Hawthorne Boulevard
Portland, OR 97214

Jump Jump Music
225 NE Broadway
Portland, OR 97232

Music Millenium
3158 East Burnside
Portland, OR 97210

PENNSYLVANIA

Third Street Jazz and Rock
20 North 3rd Street
Philadelphia, PA 19106

Jim's Records
4526 Liberty Avenue
Pittsburgh, PA 15224

SOUTH CAROLINA

Erwin Music
52½ Wentworth Street
Charleston, SC 29401

TEXAS

Sound Exchange
2100 Guadalupe
Austin, TX 78705

Waterloo
600A North Lamar Boulevard
Austin, TX 78703

VERMONT

Pure Pop Records
115 South Winooski
Burlington, VT 05401

VIRGINIA

Plan 9
104 14th Street NW, Suite 4
Charlottesville, VA 22903

Town & Campus Records
69 Liberty Street
Harrisonburg, VA 22801

WASHINGTON

Park Avenue Records
532 Queen Anne Avenue North
Seattle, WA 98109

Peaches
811 Northeast 45th Street
Seattle, WA 98105

Street Music
North 5 Wall
Spokane, WA 99201

Bibliography

BOOKS

Appleby, David P. *The Music of Brazil.* Austin, TX: University of Texas Press, 1983.

Bebey, Francis. *African Music: A People's Art.* Brooklyn, NY: Lawrence Hill Books, 1975.

Berliner, Paul F. *The Soul of Mbira.* Berkeley: University of California Press, 1978.

Chernoff, John Miller. *African Rhythm and African Sensibility.* Chicago: University of Chicago Press, 1979

Collins, John. *Music Makers of West Africa.* NY: Three Continents Press, 1985.

Coplan, David B. *In Township Tonight: South Africa's Black City Music and Theatre.* NY: Longman, 1985.

Graham, Ronnie. *The Da Capo Guide to Contemporary African Music.* NY: Da Capo Press, 1988.

Lai, T. C., and Robert Mok. *Jade Flute: The Story of Chinese Music.* NY: Schocken Books, 1985.

Malm, William P. *Music Cultures of the Pacific, the Near East, and Asia.* Englewood Cliffs, NJ: Prentice-Hall, 1977.

Nketia, J. H. K. *The Music of Africa.* NY: W. W. Norton, 1974.

Roberts, J. S. *Black Music of Two Worlds.* Tivoli, NY: Original Music, 1982.

_____. *The Latin Tinge: The Impact of Latin American Music on the United States.* Tivoli, NY: Original Music, 1985.

Sachs, Curt. *The History of Musical Instruments.* NY: W. W. Norton, 1940.

Stapleton, Chris, and Chris May. *African Rock: The Pop Music of a Continent.* NY: Obelisk/Dutton, 1990.

Thompson, Robert Farris. *Flash of the Spirit: African and Afro-American Arts and Philosophy.* NY: Vintage, 1984.

Waterman, Christopher Alan. *Juju: A Social History and Ethnography of an African Popular Music.* Chicago: University of Chicago Press, 1990.

White, Timothy. *Catch a Fire: The Life of Bob Marley.* NY: Henry Holt & Co., 1989.

Widdess, D. R., and R. F. Wolpert, eds. *Music and Tradition: Essays on Asian and Other Musics Presented to Laurence Picken.* NY: Cambridge University Press, 1981.

PERIODICALS

Africa International, published monthly, 17 rue Marguerite, 75017 Paris, France.

The Beat, published bimonthly by Bongo Productions, PO Box 65856, Los Angeles, CA 90065.

Jeune Afrique, 57 bis, Rue d'Anteuil 75016 Paris, France.

Mambo Express, Latin music newsletter, 2272 Colorado Boulevard, Los Angeles, CA 90041.

Option magazine, published by Sonic Options Network, 2345 Westwood Boulevard, #2, Los Angeles, CA 90064.

Stern's World Music Review: Tradewind, published monthly by Stern's African Music Center, 116 Whitfield Street, London W1P 5RW England.

Worldbeat, published by Lazahold Productions, Pallion Industrial Estate, Roper Street, Sunderland, England SR4 68N.